GOVERNMENT AND SOCIAL CLASS IN COLONIAL AMERICA

Titles in the series include:

LUCENT LIBRARY *of* HISTORICAL ERAS

GOVERNMENT AND SOCIAL CLASS IN COLONIAL AMERICA

DON NARDO

LUCENT BOOKS

A part of Gale, Cengage Learning

GALE
CENGAGE Learning

Detroit • New York • San Francisco • New Haven, Conn • Waterville, Maine • London

GALE
CENGAGE Learning™

LIBRARY OF CONGRESS CATALOGING-IN-PUBLICATION DATA

Nardo, Don, 1947-
  Government and social class in colonial America / by Don Nardo.
    p. cm. -- (The Lucent library of historical eras)
  Includes bibliographical references and index.
  ISBN 978-1-4205-0265-7 (hardcover)
  1. United States--History--Colonial period, ca. 1600-1775. 2. Social classes--United States--History--17th century. 3. Social classes--United States--History--18th century. I. Title.
  E188.5.N36 2010
  973.2--dc22

                                                        2009043640

Lucent Books
27500 Drake Rd.
Farmington Hills, MI 48331

ISBN-13: 978-1-4205-0265-7
ISBN-10: 1-4205-0265-4

Printed in the United States of America
1 2 3 4 5 6 7 14 13 12 11 10

Printed by Bang Printing, Brainerd, MN, 1st Ptg., 05/2010

Contents

Foreword

Looking back from the vantage point of the present, history can be viewed as a myriad of intertwining roads paved by human events. Some paths stand out—broad highways whose mileposts, even from a distance of centuries, are clear. The events that propelled the rise to power of Germany's Third Reich, its role in World War II, and its eventual demise, for example, are well defined and documented.

Other roads are less distinct, their route sometimes hidden from view. Modern legislatures may have developed from old tribal councils, for example, but the links between them are indistinct in places, open to discussion and interpretation.

The architecture of civilization—law, religion, art, science, and government—as well as the more everyday aspects of our culture—what we eat, what we wear—all developed along the historical roads and byways. In that progression can be traced every facet of modern life.

A broad look back along these roads reveals that many paths—though of vastly different character—seem to converge at a few critical junctions. These intersections are those great historical eras that echo over the long, steady course of human history, extending beyond the past and into the present.

These epic periods of time are the focus of Historical Eras. They shine through the mists of history like beacons, illuminated by a burst of creativity that propels events forward—so bright that we, from thousands of years away, can clearly see the chain of events leading to the present.

Each Historical Eras consists of a set of books that highlight various aspects of these major eras. For example, the Elizabethan England library features volumes on Queen Elizabeth I and her court, Elizabethan theater, the great playwrights, and everyday life in Elizabethan London.

The mini-library approach allows for the division of each era into its most significant and most interesting parts and the exploration of those parts in depth. Also, social and cultural trends as well as illustrative documents and eyewitness accounts can be prominently featured in individual volumes.

Historical Eras presents a wealth of information to young readers. The lively narrative, fully documented primary and secondary source quotations, maps, photographs, sidebars, and annotated bibliographies serve as launching points for class discussion and further research.

In studying the great historical eras, students also develop a better understanding of our own times. What we learn from the past and how we apply it in the present may shape the future and may determine whether our era will be a guiding light to those traveling future roads.

Introduction

SHEDDING PAST TRADITIONS AND CUSTOMS

Today it is taken for granted that the United States, as the world's oldest and largest democracy, stands for, promotes, and lives by various basic democratic principles. Among these are that all people—both male and female, young and old, and rich and poor—are equal under the law; that all have the right to aspire to wealth, happiness, and participation in government; and that all possess freedom of speech, assembly, and religion, regardless of race, ethnicity, or financial means.

It was not always this way in America, however. A common misconception is that many English and other Europeans colonized North America to escape tyranny and enjoy freedom. When a majority of people today hear the word freedom, they think about the wide range of individual freedoms that modern democracies allow. The continent's early settlers,

however, had different ideas about what freedom meant. The reality is that no liberal democratic political system resembling that of modern democracies like the United States, the United Kingdom, and France existed in colonial America.

European voyagers made the trip across the Atlantic to acquire religious freedom. In most cases, this consisted of the freedom of a particular group to worship without fear of punishment. The Puritans who established the Massachusetts Bay Colony, for instance, emigrated to America because their religious views were considered radical in Anglican England. In their new land, they were free to practice their beliefs. However, that did not mean that everyone in the colony was free to worship as he or she pleased. On the contrary, the colonists had absolutely no toleration for any religious ideas but their own and readily imprisoned or banished anyone who strayed from core Puritan beliefs.

Other English colonies, notably New York (originally the Dutch colony of New Amsterdam) and Pennsylvania, were more tolerant of other beliefs. Nevertheless, neither they nor any other English settlers who initially colonized North America's eastern seaboard came to enjoy or promote democratic politics and government. With few exceptions, the colonists were perfectly content to perpetuate the English system at first.

Rise of Representative Government

That English system certainly had democratic elements. Chief among them was the idea and practice of representative government, which allowed for a representative of a district, town, or neighborhood to sit in the national governing body. There, that person was responsible for looking after the interests of the people he represented.

During America's colonial period, England's chief governing body was Parliament (which is still the main legislature of the United Kingdom). It had developed in late medieval times out of small councils of influential lords who advised the king. It steadily grew larger and more powerful, proceeding to take over more and more governmental authority and functions that had once belonged solely to the crown. This trend reached a major climax in 1689. That year the English Bill of Rights established

that the king could not make or suspend laws, raise money, or maintain a standing army without Parliament's consent, although England (soon to become a part of Great Britain) was still considered to be a monarchy. The king (or queen) was largely a figurehead, and Parliament was truly the ruling body. This leadership structure was the foundation

The English Bill of Rights being read to Prince William and Princess Mary of England in 1689. This document essentially made the monarchy a figurehead, giving Parliament the power.

upon which a nation run by a national representative legislature without any monarchy or royalty emerged in the United States.

Rich or Poor by God's Will

In actual practice, though more inherently democratic than the governments of France and Spain during the colonial period, the English system in many ways did not resemble a democracy at all. To begin, it restricted political power and many political and social liberties to an elite few, all free males who owned land. Women, free men who had no land, indentured servants, slaves (who were rare in England) were all excluded. Moreover, the colonists had no qualms about bringing this discriminatory system with them to North America. Both in the mother country and in the colonies, noted historian Alan Taylor points out,

The higher authorities vested patriarchal [male-dominated] power in

Although women, indentured servants, and slaves shared in the work of keeping the colonies running, these people were not allowed any political power. This power was restricted to just free males who owned land.

the male heads of household. By law, only the head of the household could own land and make contracts and only male heads could vote, serve on juries, or hold political office.[1]

Even in the unusually liberal and religiously tolerant Pennsylvania, there were strict rules about who could be considered a "freeman," or citizen having the right to vote and take part in government. The "Frame of Government" for Pennsylvania, drawn up in 1782, largely by the colony's founder, William Penn, stated:

> Every inhabitant in the said province that is or shall be a purchaser of one hundred acres of land, or upwards . . . and every person who shall have paid his passage, and taken up one hundred acres of land . . . and have cultivated ten acres thereof, and . . . every [owner of land or buildings in a city] in the said province that pays "scot and lot" [special municipal taxes] to the government shall be deemed and accounted a freeman of the said province. And every such person shall, and may, be capable of electing, or being elected, representatives of the people, in provincial Council, or General Assembly, in the said province.[2]

One reason that this social system, which today seems inherently unfair, was perpetuated for so long was that most people believed it was part of the natural order of things set up by God. One of the early leaders of the Massachusetts Bay Colony, John Winthrop, famously expressed it this way: "God Almighty, in His most holy and wise providence, has so disposed of the condition of mankind, as in all times some must be rich; some poor; some high and eminent in power and dignity; others mean [ordinary] and in subjection."[3]

Growing Apart

Over time, however, this restrictive approach to politics, government, and society steadily changed. In short, it became less restrictive and more attuned to the individual needs and civil rights of ordinary citizens. One reason this happened was because the colonies were situated far from the mother country, where it was increasingly difficult for the king and Parliament to enforce their policies, or even to communicate with the colonists on a regular basis. The famous American patriot and pamphleteer, Thomas Paine, summarized this reality in his immortal *Common Sense*:

> As to government matters, it is not in the power of Britain to do this continent justice: The business of it will soon be too weighty, and intricate, to be managed with any tolerable degree of convenience, by a power so distant from us, and so very ignorant of us. For if they cannot conquer us, they cannot govern us. To be always running three or four thousand miles with a tale or

a petition, waiting four or five months for an answer, which when obtained requires five or six more to explain it in, will in a few years be looked upon as folly and childishness. There was a time when it was proper, and there is a proper time for it to cease.[4]

In addition to steadily growing apart from the mother country, the colonists underwent a change in character due to their experiences as settlers in what was for them a new and highly challenging land. The requirements and difficulties of taming a largely undeveloped continent called for fortitude and cooperation by all members of society. That included the less well off who had little or no property and were traditionally kept from determining their own destinies. Because their skills and hard work were instrumental in making the colonies successful, they came to feel that they should be rewarded for their efforts by having the same rights as other Englishmen.

At the same time, new ideas about freedom and the rights of individuals were floating around Europe in the 1600s and 1700s and inevitably found their way to the English colonies. They included not only religious toleration and freedom, but also the notion that certain basic, natural human rights existed. All people, regardless of wealth or social station, were deserving of these rights. Such ideas were not readily accepted in Europe because it was a stronghold of older, more traditional ideas that perpetuated inequality and the rule of the social elites. But in the American colonies, where European civilization was in a sense starting anew, these concepts found fertile soil in which to grow and spread.

For all of these reasons, politics, government, and social classes rapidly evolved in British America. To meet and adapt to new and unique challenges, the colonists shed many past traditions and customs that no longer seemed appropriate. In doing so, they made it inevitable that they would grow more independent from the mother country and increasingly desire to rule themselves.

Thomas Paine was the author of the famous pamphlet Common Sense, *which mentioned how the restrictive approach to politics, government, and society was changing in the American colonies.*

Chapter One

SOCIAL RANK IN BRITISH AMERICA

When the first colonists arrived in Jamestown, Plymouth, Massachusetts Bay, Maryland, and other English colonies in the 1600s, the ideal coined by Thomas Jefferson, that "all men are created equal," still lay far in the future. Indeed, in crossing the Atlantic to start new lives, the colonists largely transplanted most elements of English society directly to the new settlements. The class structure, then more often called the "social ranking" of that society, was far from equal.

The highest social rank was composed of a few wealthy landowners who together made up a small, but powerful, upper crust of aristocrats. They occupied almost all positions of power and influence in early British America. Directly below them was a relatively small middle class of well-to-do merchants. The rest, making up society's lower ranks, were small farmers, laborers, indentured servants, and slaves. Meanwhile, women formed a special social rank of their own, based on longstanding discrimination against women by men. Although an upper-class woman was seen as socially superior to both men and women in the lower classes, she was considered inferior, politically and often legally speaking, to her upper-class husband.

By custom, a colony's local aristocrats commanded a high level of respect from people in the lower social ranks. This respect for, or deference to, one's "betters" was so ingrained in society that some lower-class children were afraid to interact with upper-class individuals. As an adult, Virginian Devereaux Jarret, the son of a carpenter, recalled his upbringing:

> We were accustomed to look upon what were called *gentle folks* as beings of a superior order. For my part, I was quite shy of them, and

kept off at a humble distance. A periwig [a wig deemed fashionable by upper-class men] in those days was a distinguishing badge of gentle folk—and when I saw a man riding the road, near our house, with a wig on, it would so alarm my fears and give me such a disagreeable feeling that I dare say I would run off, as for my life. Such ideas of the differences between gentle and simple [folk] were, I believe, universal among all of my rank and age.[5]

"Better" and "Meaner" Sorts

One's social rank in colonial America's early years was signaled, or displayed, by certain distinctive factors or indicators. Chief among them were titles, or forms of address used in conversations, and the attire, or clothing, one wore on a daily basis. Regarding titles, male members of the upper class were addressed as "mister." The highest ranking of their number, usually governors or other political officials, bore the title "Esquire"; their wives were called "madam." Also, collectively speaking, upper-class people were referred to as "the better sort" or more simply as "betters." In contrast, members of the lower ranks were generally called "the meaner sort," "the common rank," or "servants."

Such titles of social rank were not merely a part of verbal exchange. They also were codified in writing and the law. In 1651 the general court of the Massachusetts Bay Colony made a plain dis-

tinction among the social ranks, referring variously to "the better class," "those above the ordinary degree," and those of "mean condition."[6]

Such divisions were deeply rooted in social custom, and especially in religious customs and beliefs. They were particularly important to the Puritans, who prided themselves in following what they believed were God's laws and wishes. Puritan leader John Winthrop not only emphasized that the social rankings were ordained by God, but also gave reasons why God wanted things to be that way. On the one hand, Winthrop believed that members of the existing upper class, to which he belonged, were dignified and good people; by placing them in charge of society, God had ensured that "wicked" rich folk would be "restrained" and thereby "the rich and mighty should not eat up [abuse and destroy] the poor." On the other hand, Winthrop said, God's system made certain that "the poor and despised [would not] rise up against their superiors and shake off their yoke [domination by said superiors]."[7]

It was only natural, therefore, according to Winthrop and other high-placed colonial leaders, for men like themselves to run society. After all, in their view God had endowed them with intellectual and moral qualities superior to those of common folk. In 1642 an argument erupted in the colony when some lower-class townsmen wanted to have equal say in some aspects of government. Winthrop stated that such an arrangement would "incur scandal by undervaluing the gifts

Puritan leader John Winthrop believed that the social rankings used in the American colonies were ordained by God.

of God." It was wholly improper, he said, for "the judgment and authority of any one of the common rank of the people [to] bear equal weight with that of the wisest and chiefest magistrate."[8]

Thus, members of the lower ranks who did not know and keep their place in the social order were seen as going against God and his master plan. Noted Puritan minister Increase Mather, born in 1639, summarized it aptly when he asked the poorer members of his flock: "You that are servants . . . have you been guilty of stubborn, disobedient carriage toward your Masters, though God in his word tells you that you ought to be obedient to them with fear and trembling?"[9]

Such disrespect for one's superiors usually resulted in punishment, such as a whipping or having to sit all day in the public stocks. In early colonial Virginia, a commoner who insulted a social superior received twenty to one hundred lashes; yet in the same colony, not only did an upper-class individual have a perfect right to insult a commoner, but also all members of the topmost social rank were exempt from whipping.

Dressing According to Status

These divisions in social rank had numerous real-life applications and consequences. For instance, in most early colonial churches, people were seated according to their social status. The local aristocrats had the best seats in the front. Indentured servants, if they were allowed to attend church at all, sat in the back.

Also, society frowned on people marrying outside their social rank. This was especially true in cases of upper-class individuals marrying persons of "mean condition." Noted Virginia aristocrat,

A painting of an upper-class colonial family exhibiting how wealthier people dressed in richer fabrics and lace trims.

Marrying Outside One's Social Rank

Many early colonial Americans felt that people should not marry outside of their social ranks. In this tract, Virginia aristocrat William Byrd II expresses his disapproval of an upper-class young woman who did so.

I learned all the tragic story of [the young woman's] humble marriage with her uncle's overseer. Besides the meanness [lowliness] of this mortal's aspect [condition], the man has not one visible qualification, except impudence, to recommend him to a [decent] female. . . . Had she run away with a gentleman or a pretty fellow, there might have been some excuse for her, though he were of inferior fortune. But to stoop to a dirty plebian [low-class person], without any kind of merit is the lowest [kind of] prostitution.

Quoted in William Byrd, *A Journey in the Land of Eden, and Other Papers.* New York: Macy-Masius, 1928, pp. 318–319.

planter, and diarist William Byrd II (1674–1744) wrote about his disdain for the marriage of a young woman of his class to a farm overseer. For her "to stoop to a dirty plebeian [lower-class person] without any kind of merit is the lowest [form of] prostitution,"[10] he said.

Even more prominent in everyday life was the relationship between social rank and dress codes. People in the upper classes were allowed to exhibit the latest fashions and to wear laces, fancy buttons, and bright colors; in general, those of lower social rank were expected to wear plainer styles and outfits with less expensive fabrics and fewer trimmings and accessories. Thus, early colonial society appears to have been far more clothes-conscious than modern society is. According to Linda Baumgarten, an expert on colonial clothing:

The story of colonial clothing is the story of people who used apparel for more than modesty or protection from the elements. They selected clothing and accessories to announce status, wealth, occupation, and personality, all within the constraining limits of the time and place. Sometimes the message was evident through the form of the garment, a hoop petticoat or a sailor's jacket, for example. More often, people relied on the nuances of fabric, tailoring, trimmings, accessories, or the accumulation of styles to speak silently on their behalf.[11]

Some early colonies actually made laws regulating what people of various social ranks could or could not wear.

This created a situation in which choosing a certain kind of attire could get a person into trouble. A 1651 Massachusetts law provided that those who dressed above their station in society must be punished. The general court declared:

> We cannot but to our grief take notice that intolerable excess and bravery [in styles of dress] has crept in upon us, and especially among people of mean condition, to the dishonor of God, [and] the scandal of our profession . . . and although we acknowledge it to be a matter of much difficulty, in regard to the blindness of men's minds and the stubbornness of their wills . . . we cannot but account it our duty to commend unto all sorts of persons the sober and moderate use of those blessings . . . the Lord has been pleased to afford unto us. . . . It is therefore ordered by this court . . . that no person in this [colony] whose visible estates, real and personal, shall not exceed [200 English pounds] shall wear any gold or silver lace, or gold and silver buttons . . . upon the penalty of ten shillings for every such offense.[12]

Dressing as Well as They Could

Colonial society was always in a state of flux, however. Just as clothing styles changed periodically, so did attitudes about social rank and dress. In the 1700s the English colonies were more populated and more sophisticated than they had been in the previous century, when their members had been preoccupied with taming the wilderness and surviving from one winter to another. Moreover, they had developed flourishing trade relations, not only with the mother country, but also with other parts of the world. The spread of trade brought more availability of many household goods, food items, and fabrics at reasonable prices.

In turn, this made it possible for folk of lower social rank to live more comfortably. As a matter of pride, many tried to appear more affluent and successful than they really were. As Alan Taylor says:

> In the new and fluid colonial societies, the display of finer consumer goods mediated claims to status. Because appearances mattered so much in regulating status and credit, colonists wished to see themselves, and to be seen by others, as something more than rude rustics.[13]

In other words, most people, regardless of social rank, tried when possible to dress as well as they could, even if that effort succeeded only in raising their own spirits and self-esteem. Even slaves tried to express themselves through their clothing, in spite of their extremely limited resources. Baumgarten writes:

Some runaway [slave] advertisements [from the 1700s] say groups of slaves were "all dressed alike" or wearing "the common dress of field slaves." Yet a careful reading of period sources shows that slaves not only desired individualized clothing but most managed to achieve it, to exert a measure of control over their appearance. Scholarship has shown that slaves enhanced their appearance and expressed personality by such techniques as styling the hair, wearing a large kerchief as a head wrap, dyeing clothing, purchasing or trading for pieces of clothing, wearing garments in new combinations, or adding pockets or patches. Was [the runaway slave] Fanny's petticoat "very much patched" because it was worn, or had she, perhaps, deliberately added decorative patches? The possibility is that what a white slaveholder viewed as a profusion of mending patches was, in the eyes of the woman who wore the petticoat, a purposeful assemblage of aesthetically [artistically] pleasing color and pattern on an otherwise plain garment.[14]

Nevertheless, serious efforts to dress to impress others in later colonial times were limited mainly to city dwellers and

Changing Fashions and Social Rank

Clothing styles, which made important statements of social rank in England's colonies, could change rapidly, often dictated by emerging London fashions, as pointed out by William Eddis, an Englishman who settled in the colonies in 1769.

The quick importation of fashions from the mother country is really astonishing. I am almost inclined to believe that a new fashion is adopted earlier by the polished and affluent Americans, than by many opulent [rich] persons in the great metropolis [London]. Nor are op-

portunities wanted [lacking] to display superior elegance. We have varied amusements and numerous parties, which afford to the young [and] the ambitious an extensive field to contend in the race of vain and idle [social] competition. In short, very little difference is in reality observable in the manners of the wealthy colonist and the wealthy Briton. Good and bad habits prevail on both sides of the Atlantic.

William Eddis, *Letters from America*. London: C. Dilly, 1792, pp. 112–113.

members of the merchant and upper classes. Throughout most of the 1700s, farmers in the countryside had no qualms about dressing in traditional farmers' working attire. According to historian John C. Miller:

> Instead of wigs, they [farmers] wore their hair long and tied in the back with a ribbon. If they wore buckles on their shoes, they were of brass [rather than gold or silver]. Instead of lace, they used a plain linen neckband. And instead of breeches and pumps [commonly worn by the wealthy], they wore trousers, homespun stockings, and cowhide shoes.[15]

The Props of Gentility

Meanwhile, as some of the surface distinctions between the upper and lower classes continued to blur as the 1700s wore on, the traditional aristocrats searched for new ways to assert their social preeminence. The object became to appear as "genteel," or refined, polished, and superior, as possible. One way to display such gentility was through a more substantial display of wealth than mere fancy attire. The well-to-do could afford to build more lavish homes than people in the lower classes could, for example. Yet throughout most of the 1600s, a majority of high-ranking individuals had lived in small, cramped, unpainted wooden houses like everyone else in the early colonies.

In the eighteenth century, by contrast, many members of the upper class erected larger homes, quite often of red brick. These had both more and larger rooms; elegant moldings, banisters, and other decorations; expensive desks, hutches, chairs, and other fine furniture items; and extensive, manicured grounds. One of the most conspicuous examples was Westover (near Williamsburg, Virginia), built in 1730, by the same William Byrd who looked down on marriage outside of one's class. According to its modern curators:

> The house is considered one of the most outstanding examples of Georgian architecture in America. Of special notice are the unusual steepness of the roof [and] the tall chimneys in pairs at both ends. Another special touch is the elaborate doorway, which continues to be recognized as "the Westover doorway" despite its adaptation to many other buildings. The special charm of the house lies in its elegant yet extremely simple form and proportions, combined with its perfect setting in the landscape, the essence of the artistic ideals of its period adapted to the style of living in Colonial Virginia.[16]

Yet as society as a whole gained increasing access to more, and in some cases finer, consumer goods, at least some members of the lower classes attempted to compete with their "betters." As Taylor phrases it, such social climbers strove, as consumers, to efface [get rid of] the insulting line between gentility and commonality. Indeed, maintaining gentility required constant expense and attention to fashion, for the middling sort [middle and lower classes] blurred the distinction by stretching their budgets to buy some of the props of gentility. Rather than accept inferiority, artisan and farm families wanted to sip tea from ceramic teacups—because the elite did so.[17]

The rich and powerful naturally looked down on what they saw as disrespectful attempts by inferiors to climb beyond their God-given place on the social ladder. Not surprisingly, some members of the genteel class spoke out to condemn such efforts. In 1744 Virginia's Dr. Alexander Hamilton (who was not related to the later founding father) wrote: "If luxury was to be confined to the rich alone, it might prove a great national good." Hamilton had recently traveled throughout the English colonies.

Built in 1730, William Byrd's mansion of Westover Plantation near Williamsburg, Virginia, remains the most outstanding example of an upper-class colonial home in the United States.

The New American Aristocracy

The colonial aristocracy that William Byrd represented was made up of well-to-do men who fancied themselves equal to the leaders of society back in England. Those leaders did not always see it that way. It was common to view colonial aristocrats as a step below aristocrats in the mother country. No matter how others saw them, Byrd and his fellows occupied an important position—a social and political bridge between the leadership in England and the general populace of ordinary colonists, as explained by scholar Alexander O. Boulton:

Williams Byrd was [born] in Virginia [and] by his fiftieth birthday he had spent more time in London than in the colonies. . . . He read or spoke at least five languages and counted dukes and earls among his friends. . . . In Virginia [he] was, in fact, one of the founding members of a new American aristocracy. [His] social standing was just below that of the governor [in Virginia]. Byrd's life history, with slight differences in detail, was mirrored in the histories of other owners of Georgian houses [in British America, who] all played similar roles as middlemen between rude colonial settlements and the splendors of the imperial capital. Caught between two worlds in the years before the Revolution, they were the leaders who first tried to regulate and direct the rising tensions between colonists and king.

Alexander O. Boulton, "The Best of Georgian." American Heritage. www.americanheritage.com/articles/magazine/ah/1989/1/1989_1_110.shtml.

William Byrd was a member of the colonial aristocracy and occupied the important position of social and political bridge between the leadership in England and ordinary middle-class and lower-class colonists.

He was appalled to see fine furniture and tableware and other expensive items in the modest houses of a number of farmers and workers. One farmhouse, he complained, had "superfluous [unnecessary] things which showed an inclination to finery . . . such as a looking glass with a painted frame, half a dozen pewter spoons, and as many plates . . . a set of stone tea dishes, and a teapot." In his view, it was more socially fitting for farmers to use "wooden plates and spoons." Also, "a little water in a wooden pail might serve for a looking glass."[18]

Hamilton and other colonial aristocrats clearly hated any attempt by lower-class individuals to aspire to higher social status than what they had been born into. One way the wealthy reacted was to become still bigger consumers of expensive goods than before. The result was a sort of ongoing contest among the social classes that caused people of all walks of life to buy more than they could afford. Consequently, large numbers of colonists in the mid-1700s were in debt, despite the fact that British America was highly prosperous overall. "Our importation of dry goods from England is so vastly great," New Yorker William Smith stated in 1762, "that we are obliged to [try everything we can think of] to [pay back] the British merchants."[19] Interestingly, this tendency toward high consumer debt was one way that late colonial American society closely resembled its modern American counterpart.

Chapter Two

DEVELOPMENT OF COLONIAL GOVERNMENT

From their beginnings, England's North American colonies sought effective ways to govern themselves. Each did so in its own way, and no two colonial governments were exactly alike. Yet, they did exhibit certain similarities that allow them to be grouped into convenient categories.

Modern historians usually divide the early colonies into two general types—corporate and royal. Corporate colonies (which are sometimes referred to as either charter or proprietary colonies) were those that were owned and run by private interests. These ranged from wealthy individuals, to influential families, to corporations and other companies. Virginia (initially Jamestown) was first established by a joint stock company, the Virginia Company, for example. Maryland was founded by a rich landowner and his family. In contrast, royal colonies (also

called provincial colonies) were owned and run by the British crown.

Most of the colonies were initially corporate. The British government gave them charters, or official documents granting them permission to set up their privately-run colonies. In time, however, the crown revoked most of the charters and transformed the formerly corporate colonies into royal colonies. Rhode Island and Connecticut were the only ones that retained their original charters right up to the American Revolution.

The difference between corporate and royal colonies had a major bearing on the way these settlements were governed. Once established, corporate colonies enjoyed fairly extensive autonomy, or independence, from the mother country. So, they were free to choose their political leaders in ways they felt best suited their needs. When they converted to royal colonies, however, the British government assumed a stronger and more direct role in colonial politics.

Setting Up a Corporate Colony

To understand how colonial governments changed over time, one must first look at how the initial corporate colonies organized and ran themselves. Although they were controlled by private individuals or companies, those people and groups had no legal right to simply sail to North America and set up a colony anywhere they wanted. In the legal theory of that time, a European monarch had authority over any overseas lands that one of his or her explorers claimed in the name of the crown. He or she could then grant use of some of those lands to various persons or groups. Such a grant, giving official permission to form a new settlement, became known as a charter.

The charters granted by English kings and queens were extremely formal documents. As such, they were filled with legal terminology and flowery language and written in long, rambling sentences, so the originals are difficult to read today. Following is the opening section of the Plymouth Colony's charter, with modernized spellings and punctuation:

To all to whom these presents shall come, greetings. Whereas our late sovereign, King James, for the advancement of a colony and plantation in the country . . . known by the name of New England, in America, by his highness's [authority] in the eighteenth year of his [reign] did give [his permission] to [a long list follows of the men who applied for the charter] and their successors that they should be one body politic and corporate [entity] consisting of forty persons, and that they . . . and their successors should be incorporated, called, and known by the name of the Council Established at Plymouth in the county of Devon for the planting, ruling, [organizing], and governing of New England, in America . . . forever under the reservations, limitations, and declarations [stated in this charter].[20]

The charters did not necessarily say how the governments of the colonies should be structured. Rather, they mainly gave the leaders of the expeditions the authority to run the colonies in the most expedient and efficient manner they could. However, some indications of what future colonial governments would look like came from the Mayflower Compact. A relatively short document, it was drafted and signed by the Plymouth colonists shortly after they arrived in Massachusetts. What makes it noteworthy is that it conceives that government should be fair, equitable, and structured and run by mutual consent,

Plymouth colonists signing the Mayflower Compact shortly after arriving in Massachusetts in 1620.

or the will of the majority. As such, it was the first political document in the Americas written by the people that the document would govern.

It says:

We whose names are under-written, the loyal subjects of our dread sovereign Lord, King James . . . having undertaken, for the glory of God, and advancement of the Christian faith, and honor of our King and Country, a voyage to plant the first colony in the northern parts of [North America], do [solemnly] combine ourselves together into a civil body politic, for our better ordering and preservation and furtherance of the ends aforesaid; and by virtue hereof to enact, constitute, and frame such just and equal laws, ordinances, acts, constitutions and offices, from time to time, as shall be thought most meet and convenient for the general good of the Colony, unto which we promise all due submission and obedience. In witness whereof we have hereunder subscribed our names at Cape Cod . . . in the year [1620].[21]

A Private Empire

By comparison, such legal equality among the first settlers was far from the minds of those who established the initial Maryland colony. The crown granted its initial charter to a wealthy individual, Lord Baltimore. (The first Lord Baltimore, George Calvert, died shortly before the charter became official. His son Caecilius, the second Lord Baltimore, and another son, Leonard, actually established the colony.)

The terms of the charter were so broad and generous that at first, the entire colony was the Calvert family's private property—in a way a private empire. In many aspects, the deal resembled the ones in which medieval kings gave estates to feudal lords who then ruled over subservient populations of oppressed peasants. The following section of the charter gives Lord Baltimore and his heirs the authority to run the colony and make and enforce its laws in any ways they see fit:

The charter for the initial Maryland colony was granted to Lord Baltimore, George Calvert, but he died before the charter became official.

Now [Lord] Baltimore [is] the true lord and proprietary of the whole province [of Maryland]. Know ye therefore further, that *We [i.e., the king]*, for Us, our Heirs and Successors, *do grant unto the said [Lord Baltimore]* (in whose fidelity, prudence, [and] justice [We have] the greatest Confidence) *and to his Heirs, [the authority] to ordain, make, and enact laws, of what kind whatsoever, according to their sound discretion,* within that and [of Maryland], and the sea of those parts, and in such form as to the said [Lord Baltimore] or his Heirs shall seem most fitting. [Italics added to emphasize the king's di-

rect grant of nearly absolute powers to the Calverts.][22]

At first, as might be expected, the Calvert family was extremely powerful and dominated local politics. Over time, other members of the community felt oppressed and agitated and expressed a desire for a larger say in the colony's affairs. As one modern expert puts it:

By 1650, opponents of the proprietor secured the right to organize a

Electing Leaders in Connecticut

In 1635 some settlers from the Massachusetts Bay Colony ventured out on their own and established a new colony in what is now Connecticut. Three years later, they drew up the "Fundamental Orders of Connecticut," a basic blueprint for the initial government of the colony. As one of the first written constitutions in the Americas, it later earned Connecticut the nickname of "the Constitution state." Connecticut also was one of only two English colonies in which public officials were elected by the people from the beginning. This section of the "Orders" deals with the manner of electing major political leaders, or magistrates:

It is ordered, sentenced and decreed, that the election of [the] magistrates shall be on this manner: Every person present and qualified for choice shall bring in . . . one single paper with the name of him written in it whom he desires to have Governor, and he that has the greatest number of papers shall be Governor for that year. And the rest of the magistrates or public officers to be chosen in this manner: The Secretary for the time being shall first read the names of all that are to be put to choice [i.e., all those nominated] and every one that would have the person nominated to be chosen shall bring in one single paper written upon, and he that would not have him chosen shall bring in a blank. And every one that has more written papers than blanks shall be a magistrate for that year.

"Fundamental Orders of Connecticut." Lonang Library. www.lonang.com/exlibris/organic/1639-foc2.htm.

lower house of the legislature, and this assembly became the center of opposition to the Calvert family. Assemblymen frequently protested the extent of Lord Baltimore's powers and complained about his policies [and] struggled for political dominance.[23]

Eventually, the needs of a rapidly changing society allowed a more representative government to develop in Maryland. Consequently, the founder's family lost control.

Colonial Governors and Advisory Councils

Whatever governmental structures the various colonies chose to implement, they all bore some similarities, both to one another and to the political system back in England. Even though they left the mother country and moved to North America, all of the colonists still considered themselves to be Englishmen. They were used to a certain kind of political system with specific sorts of leaders. It was only natural that they would incorporate some of those familiar concepts into their own new systems.

Each colony needed an overall leader or governor—a chief executive to oversee the elements of government. What differed from colony to colony was not the office of governor, but the manner in which the person in that office was chosen. Only in Connecticut and Rhode Island were the governors elected by

eligible voters, foreshadowing the more democratic system that would later be adopted by the U.S. founding fathers. The following clause of Connecticut's frame of government (the "Fundamental Orders"), drawn up in 1638, provides for yearly elections and describes those eligible to vote:

It is ordered, sentenced and decreed, that there shall be yearly two general assemblies or courts, the one the second Thursday in April . . . called the Court of Election, wherein shall be yearly chosen [so] many magistrates and other public officers as shall be found requisite [needed], one to be chosen governor for the year ensuing and . . . no other magistrate to be chosen for more than one year. [That governor] shall have power to administer justice according to the laws here established, and [the] choice [of that leader] shall be made by all that are admitted freemen and have taken the oath of fidelity, and do cohabit [live] within this jurisdiction [i.e., the towns making up the Connecticut Colony].[24]

In most other colonies, by contrast, governors were appointed. In a majority of the early corporate colonies, such appointments were made by the proprietors—either persons or companies—of said colonies. When these colonies later became royal provinces, the governors were appointed by the king (assisted by

A meeting of the House of Lords, one of two houses of Parliament in England. The advisory councils found in American colonial government were similar to the House of Lords.

his advisers). A royal governor was, in a sense, the monarch's deputy, charged with looking after his and Britain's interests in the colony. Eventually, nearly all of the colonies had royal governors. A noted scholar of U.S. history, Bernard Bailyn, summarizes their weighty duties:

> As the chief representatives of Britain, governors were responsible for enforcing British trade laws and carrying out other directives [of the king and Parliament]. As chief executives, governors were responsible for executing colonial laws, administering justice, and appointing most administrative and judicial officers. As commanders in chief, they were responsible for provincial defense and diplomatic relations with the Indians and the other colonies. As one of three branches of the legislature, they had veto power over all laws and took an active role in the legislative process.[25]

Directly below the governor in most colonial governments was his advisory council. As indicated by that term, the people on the council advised the governor on a wide range of matters. In certain ways, the advisory council was similar to the House of Lords back in England. (The House of Lords, often called just "the Lords," was one of the two houses of Parliament; the other was the House of Commons, or "the Commons.") Like the Lords did for the Commons and king, a colonial advisory council gave its approval to the colonial governor's important decisions. Also, the governor's advisers' consent was usually needed for the passage of laws.

The members of colonial advisory councils were chosen in different ways. In Connecticut and Rhode Island, they were elected by the people, as governors and other public officials were. In three other early colonies the advisers were chosen by the members of the local assembly, or legislature. In the rest, either the proprietor or the king appointed the advisers.

Popular Assemblies and Local Government

The assemblies that chose the advisers (sometimes called the "lower houses" of colonial governments) were in many ways the equivalents of the House of Commons in Britain. Members of the Commons represented various towns and districts across Britain. Similarly, the members of a colonial assembly represented the people in various parts of the colony. Through such assemblies, ordinary colonists conveyed their grievances and political likes, dislikes, and demands to the people in power.

These small legislatures were the chief lawmaking bodies of the colonies. Members debated and voted on new laws similarly to the way that members of the Commons did (and members of the U.S. House of Representatives do today). However, any new law proposed by a

Local Government in New England

The late American historian Henry W. Elson penned this overview of local government in the New England colonies.

In methods of local government the colonies were less uniform than in the general government.... The old parish of England became the town in New England. The people, owing to the necessity of guarding against the Indians and wild animals, and to their desire to attend the same church, settled in small, compact communities, or townships, which they called towns. The town was a legal corporation [and] was the political unit.... It was a democracy of the purest type. Several times a year the adult males met in town meetings to discuss public questions, to lay taxes, to make local laws, and to elect officers. The chief officers were the "selectmen," from three to nine in number, who should have the general management of the public business. [To] this day the town government continues in a large measure in some parts of New England. The county in New England was of much less importance than the town. Its business was chiefly the holding of courts of law, the keeping of court records, and the care of prisoners.

Henry W. Elson, *History of the United States of America.* New York: Macmillan, 1941, pp. 214–215.

---

colonial assembly had to be approved by the governor's advisory council. In addition, the governor could veto it at his discretion. A more crucial power vested in the assembly was connected to an always controversial issue—taxation. The local legislature had to give its consent to any proposed new taxes that might be levied by the governor or English Parliament.

The oldest and arguably most famous of these colonial assemblies was Virginia's House of Burgesses, informally known as "the Burgesses." (The term burgess originally meant a free man living in a local English district. In time, it came to mean a representative of that district in the legislature.) Established in 1619, it was the first formal legislative body in the Americas. It initially met in Jamestown; later, in 1699, it moved to Virginia's new capital of Williamsburg.

At first the Burgesses was made up only of a few local officials and prominent colonists. But in 1624 the Virginia Company, the proprietor of the colony, lost its charter and Jamestown became a royal colony. Thereafter, the assembly consisted of two men (women were not allowed to serve in government) from each county in the colony and one man each from Williamsburg, Jamestown, Norfolk, and the College of William and

Mary. Each of these men was elected by his constituents, those citizens he represented. Because of the extensive authority possessed by royal governors and their advisers, the powers of the House of Burgesses, like those of most other colonial legislatures, were rather limited for a long time. Only in the mid-1700s did these assemblies begin to assert themselves more aggressively and to overtly defy the mother country.

Below the colony-wide officials and legislature in each colony were extensive elements of local government. As in England, local elected justices of the peace administered justice, aided by small local courts. In some colonies, including New York and North Carolina, the county was the central unit of local government. In South Carolina and Georgia, in contrast, it was the parish (a geographical area populated by members of a local church). In the New England colonies, the town was the basic local governmental unit. Elected town officials were (and still are) known as selectmen. All across New England there were annual town meetings in which citizens showed up to discuss and vote on local issues. (Such town meetings are still an important fixture of local government in the region.)

The colonial electorates, composed of the citizens who voted in local meetings and elected the assembly members, were long a privileged minority. Most societal

Authority to Govern the Colony

The following section of the charter of the Massachusetts Bay Colony gives the leaders of the expedition authority to run the colony as they see fit and to defend it in any way necessary against assault by outside forces:

And we do further, for us, our heirs and successors, give and grant to the said governor and company, and their successors . . . full and absolute power and authority to correct, punish, pardon, govern, and rule all such the subjects of us, our heirs and successors, as shall from time to time adventure themselves in any voyage. . . .

And we do further [give] and grant to the said Governor and Company and their successors . . . [the authority] for their special defense and safety, to encounter, expel, repel, and resist by force of arms, as well by sea as by land, and by all fitting ways and means whatsoever, all such person and persons, as shall at any time hereafter, attempt or enterprise the destruction, invasion, detriment, or annoyance to the said plantation or inhabitants.

"Charter of Massachusetts Bay Colony." Lonang Library. www.lonang.com/exlibris/organic/1629-cmb2.htm.

A meeting of the House of Burgesses in Jamestown, Virginia, in 1619. This group became the first elected legislative assembly in America.

groups, including women, indentured servants, slaves, and men who did not own property, were completely excluded.

Only free white males with property could vote or hold public office. Since property was relatively easy to obtain with only a minimal amount of money, an estimated 80 to 90 percent of free white males in each colony could vote.

Social Elites and Vast Distances

Even though a fair number of colonists could vote, the colonies were still not very democratic by modern standards.

This was mainly because of the money and influence of the social elites, especially the wealthy landowners. As historian Irwin Unger points out:

Although local political bodies in the colonies developed many popular elements, they also retained much of the aristocratic quality of England. Southern [colonial leaders] appointed their own successors and were dominated by the [clique] of rich planters who resembled the country gentry of England. Southern country government was too aristocratic, with country justices, sheriffs and coroners normally appointed by the royal governor. Nor was the town, the basic governmental unit in New England, entirely democratic. The town meeting admitted virtually all adult males . . . but community leaders did not readily tolerate dissent. . . . Democracy did not exist in the seventeenth and eighteenth centuries, and democracy was not a positive word in the colonial vocabulary. It was almost equivalent to anarchy. . . . Not until the revolutionary era [the 1760s and 1770s] did democratic rhetoric [speech and discussion] become commonplace.[26]

One major reason that the colonial governments did eventually assume larger authority and become more democratic was the great size of the Atlantic Ocean. The simple fact that the colonies and mother country were separated by vast distances proved to have far-reaching consequences. Over time, the two societies grew apart. The colonists increasingly felt that they, and not faraway kings and politicians they had never met, should decide their destinies.

Chapter Three

THE IMPACT OF BACON'S REBELLION

I n the mid-to-late 1600s, the rapidly evolving societies and governments of many of the colonies encountered various internal crises that brought them perilously close to the brink of collapse. In some cases, armed rebellions broke out. Local leaders felt they had no other choice but to appeal to the English king for aid. In other incidences, Indian wars ravaged the frontiers, spreading fear and chaos.

For its part, the British government had long been searching for more effective and lucrative ways to exploit the colonies. It had not been very successful, though, because most colonies were privately run, as granted in their original charters. More and more, however, the king and leaders of Parliament saw the mounting troubles in the colonies as a convenient excuse to step in and assert more direct control. Between the 1680s and 1730s, the British government did, in fact, revoke most of the colonial charters. These former corporate colonies now became full-fledged royal colonies with British-appointed governors who reported directly to the crown.

The most famous and far-reaching of the crises the colonies experienced in this period was Bacon's Rebellion, which was nothing less than a regional civil war. Often misleadingly called a precursor to the American Revolution, coincidentally it took place in 1676, exactly one hundred years before the larger insurrection that created the United States. The earlier revolt, led by a popular, charismatic Virginia colonist named Nathaniel Bacon, and other violent events in the same period had serious consequences for colonial governments and societies. Basically, the British government's intervention in North America and creation of many royal colonies made the former corporate colonies far less independent. As one of the leading scholars of Bacon's Rebellion, Stephen S. Webb, puts it:

> In 1676, the American colonies lost—and lost for a century to come—their independence. It had been well established. The colonies had first asserted their governmental autonomy in the later 1630s. With varying success, they had defended their political freedom against the English commonwealth. [They] had mostly governed themselves. Then, in 1676, a [combination] of disasters [ended that situation]. Civil war [and other explosive incidents] shattered the colonial oligarchies [existing groups of leaders]. In this crisis, many of the American colonists rejected the rule of their autonomous elites and either sought or had forced upon them the administrative attention of the English state.[27]

The Opposing Leaders

It is important to stress that Nathaniel Bacon was not a classic freedom fighter trying to defeat tyranny and bring liberty to the people. "Although Bacon attacked a royal governor," Alan Taylor explains, "he did not seek independence from England." Indeed, "proclaiming their loyalty to England, Bacon and his supporters insisted that they acted only against a corrupt governor who had betrayed the king." Moreover, the rebellion was essentially a mini civil war, "a division within the planter elite [of Virginia], a split between a [group] allied with the royal governor and a rival set of ambitious but frustrated planters."[28]

Of the leaders of the opposing sides in the dispute, the first, Bacon, was a young man in his late twenties but already fairly well accomplished in life. A contemporary Virginian and one of the earliest American-born historians, Robert Beverley, wrote an account of the rebellion in 1704, in which he described Bacon. (Because Beverley sympathized with the royal governor, rather than Bacon, the picture he draws of Bacon is somewhat unflattering.)

> This gentleman [Bacon] had been brought up [in a well-to-do home] in England, and had a moderate fortune. He was young, bold, active, and [had] powerful elocution [speaking abilities]. In a word, he was in every way qualified to head a giddy and unthinking multitude. Before he had been three years in the country, he was, for his extraordinary qualifications, made one of the [governor's] council, and in great honor and esteem among the people. For this reason he no sooner gave countenance to this riotous mob, but they all presently fixed their eyes upon him for their general [leader] and accordingly made their addresses to him.[29]

On the other side of the conflict was the royal governor, William Berkeley. Now in his sixties, he had administered

Rebel leader Nathaniel Bacon confronting royal governor William Berkeley in colonial Virginia. Although Bacon attacked Berkeley he was not attempting to free Virginia from England, but only from what he saw as a corrupt governor.

the colony for three decades, mostly in a high-handed manner dictated by his personal whims. He was also quite rich, with a salary of a thousand English pounds per year. (At the time, a small farmer in Virginia was lucky to make three pounds net profit per year above his overhead and expenses.) Berkeley had no qualms about promoting the interests of other wealthy individuals, some of whom were friends he placed in powerful governmental positions. An example of his haughty, elitist character comes through in a 1671 public statement in which he disparaged the notions of freedom of the press and public education for average people:

I thank God there are no free schools, nor printing [in Virginia], and I hope we shall not have these [for a] hundred years. For learning has brought disobedience and heresy . . . into the world, and printing has divulged them [to the people]. God keep us from both![30]

Bacon's Grievances

Whatever Berkeley's shortcomings as a governor and as a man, he was very adept at perpetuating the status quo and keeping the peace with local Indian tribes. His Indian policy consisted of avoiding conflicts with the tribes, in part,

Berkeley Denounces Bacon

The governor of Virginia, William Berkeley, issued a declaration, excerpted here, calling Nathaniel Bacon a treasonous rebel and pointing out that he had given Bacon every chance to do the right thing before having to denounce him.

My most assured friends, I would have preserved those Indians that I knew were hourly at our mercy, [and acted as] our spies and intelligence, to find out our bloody enemies [rather than kill them as Bacon did]. . . . To conclude, I have done what was possible both to friend and enemy, have granted Mr. Bacon three pardons, which he has scornfully rejected, supposing himself stronger to subvert [the laws] [than] I and you to maintain the laws. . . . I will add no more, though much more is still remaining to justify me and condemn Mr. Bacon, but to desire that this declaration may be read in every County Court in the Country, and that a Court be presently called to do it, before the Assembly meet. . . . Let all [the king's] good subjects say Amen.

William Berkeley, *The Declaration and Remonstrance of Sir William Berkeley, His Most Sacred Majesties' Governor and Captain General of Virginia.* Available at: http://odur.let.rug.nl/~usa/D/1651-1700/bacon_rebel/berke.htm.

Colonists defending themselves from Native American attacks. Bacon and his followers objected to Berkeley's response after the Susquehannock tribe began to attack colonial settlers on the Virginia frontier.

by preserving existing borders between white and Indian lands. Whenever possible, Berkeley curbed attempts by land-hungry settlers to seize Indian lands to build new farms and towns. He also cultivated a degree of friendship with some tribes, especially the Pamunkey, who helped the whites gather useful intelligence against less friendly tribes.

Bacon and his followers objected to these policies, particularly after hostilities erupted on the western Virginia frontier in 1675. Three white settlers were killed by Indians, probably members of the Susquehannock tribe. A squad of Virginia militia (farmers who doubled as part-time soldiers) went out to search for the culprits and encountered a large group of Susquehannock camped on the Potomac River. An unfortunate series of incidents followed. As noted historian Samuel E. Morison tells it:

The Indians sent out five chiefs to parley. An angry [argument] took place with the white officers, at the end of which the five chiefs were taken away and killed, by whose order

The Governor Labeled a Traitor

In his manifesto, Bacon demanded that Berkeley and his leading followers surrender. If they did not, Bacon and his own followers would treat them as traitors to the colony.

We do further demand that the said Sir William Berkeley with all the persons in this list be forthwith delivered up or surrender themselves within four days after the notice hereof, or otherwise we declare as follows: That in whatsoever place, house, or ship, any of the said persons shall reside, be hidden, or protected, we declare the owners [of] the said places to be confederates and traitors to the people and the estates of them [will] be confiscated, and this we the commons of Virginia do declare, desiring a firm union amongst ourselves that we may jointly and with one accord defend ourselves against the common enemy, and let not the faults of the guilty be the reproach of the innocent, or the faults or crimes of the oppressors divide and separate us who have suffered by their oppressions.

Nathaniel Bacon, *The Declaration of the People.* Available at: http://odur.let.rug.nl/~usa/D/1651-1700/bacon_rebel/bacon.htm.

is uncertain. That unjust act, contrary to [accepted rules of diplomacy and war], sparked off an Indian war. The embittered Susquehannock broke into roving bands that attacked one plantation after another on the Virginia frontier.[31]

Berkeley reacted to these attacks in his usual cautious manner. He was well aware that a large Indian war involving most of the tribes in New England was then raging a few hundred miles north of Virginia. He did not want to risk igniting a similar all-out conflict in his own region, so he adopted the defensive strategy of erecting nine forts on the frontier, hoping these would discourage the Susquehannock raiders.

A number of settlers and planters on Virginia's frontier were appalled at the governor's approach to the crisis. One remarked that Berkeley "does not take a speedy course to destroy the Indians" because of "his love [of] the beaver."[32] This charge referred to the fact that Berkeley was heavily involved in the ongoing lucrative trade in beaver furs with various Indian groups. Whatever the governor's motives, many white inhabitants of the frontier region saw the Indians as little better than vermin and wanted them to be put down hard, even exterminated if possible. They found a willing leader in Nathaniel Bacon, who abhorred the natives.

Bacon had other grievances against the local governor besides his Indian policy. Berkeley's tax policies benefited only the richest planters, most of whom were actually tax exempt, Bacon pointed out. Also, the governor placed mainly his close friends in high government positions, passing over other worthy planters. Bacon also charged Berkeley with monopolizing the fur trade.

The Rebellion Begins

Bacon's insurrection started shortly after he demanded to be allowed to lead a band of militia in a punitive raid against the Indians. Although Berkeley did not want to inflame the already strained relations between the colonists and Indians, at the same time he did not like the idea of giving command of the colony's armed forces to someone he neither agreed with, nor trusted. Ultimately, he discouraged Bacon from trying to punish the Susquehannock.

Bacon proceeded to ignore the governor, gathered some armed men, and went on the attack. These colonial avengers were highly indiscriminate in choosing their targets, however. Thoughtlessly, they assaulted and slew a number of friendly Indians, which, just as Berkeley had feared, made relations far worse.

Under pressure from a number of planters and eager to diffuse tensions among the factions in the colony, Berkeley pardoned Bacon for his rash actions. Still, Bacon refused to let matters rest. He now demanded that the governor and assembly grant him a formal commission (military rank and authority to make war). When it looked like this demand would be refused, Bacon resorted to intimidation. According to Beverley's account:

Having put himself at the head of six hundred volunteers, [Bacon] marched directly to Jamestown, where the assembly was then sitting. He presented himself before the assembly, and drew up his men in battalions before the house wherein they sat. He [told the lawmakers] that if the commission had not been delayed [for] so long, the war against the Indians might [already] have been finished. The governor resented this insolent [display] and now obstinately refused to grant him anything.... But the assembly, fearing the fatal consequences of provoking [Bacon and his armed men, who had] the governor, council, and assembly entirely in their power, [urged] the governor to grant Bacon his request. They prepared themselves the commission, [giving him the title of] general of the forces of Virginia, and brought it to the governor to be signed. With much reluctance, the governor signed it, and thereby put the power of war and peace into Bacon's hands.[33]

Satisfied, Bacon gathered his men and headed back toward the frontier, determined to slaughter as many Indians as he could. As soon as he felt Bacon was far enough away from Jamestown, Berkeley issued a decree calling him a traitor and rebel. The following excerpt from the document stresses that Bacon is not a man of the people and accuses him of committing treason:

Now I will state the question between me as a governor and Mr. Bacon. . . . [His taking up arms] is treason, for the [recent] event [in Jamestown] showed that whatever the pretence was to seduce ignorant and well affected people, yet the end was ruinous both to King and people, as this [situation] will be if not prevented. I do therefore again declare that Bacon, proceeding against all laws of all nations, modern and ancient, is [a] rebel to his sacred Majesty and this country. . . . Now my friends I have lived 34 years

Rebel leader Nathaniel Bacon demanding his commission from royal governor William Berkeley in colonial Virginia in 1676.

amongst you, as uncorrupt and diligent as ever [a] governor was. Bacon is a man of two years amongst you, his person and qualities unknown to most of you, and to all men else, by any virtuous action that ever I heard of. And that very action which he boasts of [attacking the Indians], was sickly and foolishly, [and] treacherously carried [out] to the dishonor of the English nation. In it, he lost more men [than] I did in three years [of] war. . . . Mr. Bacon has none about him but the lowest of the people.[34]

Jamestown in Flames

The governor's decree did not frighten Bacon, who appeared confident that he had the supporters and resources needed to take over the colony. He very nearly succeeded. Hoping to turn more farmers and other colonists against Berkeley and the government in Jamestown, he issued a statement condemning the governor's policies, particularly those involving the Indians. Sometimes referred to as "Bacon's Manifesto," it reads in part:

> [We oppose Governor Berkeley] for having protected, favored, and emboldened the Indians against his Majesty's loyal subjects, never [enacting] any due or proper means of satisfaction for their many invasions, robberies, and murders committed upon us. . . . When the army of English was just upon the track

of those Indians, who now in all places burn, spoil, murder, and when we might with ease have destroyed them, [Berkeley] expressly countermanded and sent back our army, by passing his word for the peaceable [treatment] of the said Indians, who immediately prosecuted their evil intentions, committing [horrible] murders and robberies in all places, being protected by the . . . word [of] Sir William Berkeley, having ruined and laid desolate a great part of his Majesty's country, [and as a result] we accuse Sir William Berkeley as guilty of [having] traitorously attempted, violated, and injured his Majesty's interest here, by a loss of a great part of this his colony and many of his faithful, loyal subjects, by him betrayed and in a barbarous and shameful manner exposed to the incursions and murder of the heathen [godless Indian].[35]

Bacon's appeal to ordinary colonists, many of whom disliked and feared all Indians, was effective, and he gained large numbers of followers. There were, however, still a fair number of loyalists—those who supported Berkeley's regime. To ensure that his own supporters remained true to the cause, Bacon demanded they swear an oath of loyalty to him. He also confiscated the lands and belongings of several prominent loyalists, which sent a message to others who dared to continue backing Berkeley. Bacon also

Unhappy with royal governor William Berkeley's policies regarding Native Americans, a group of Virginia rebels led by Nathaniel Bacon set fire to Jamestown in protest.

boldly captured two government-owned ships on the James River and turned them into a small, but effective, rebel navy. Finally, the rebels marched on Jamestown and burned most of it to the ground. "The general of the revolution himself," Webb writes,

> put the torch to Virginia's mother church, the sacred support of royal authority. [Meanwhile] humbler rebels rejoiced as they burned the homes and offices of their oppressors. . . . Governor Berkeley's five houses, worth, with their contents, 6,000 [English pounds], twenty gentlemen's mansions, and other symbols of authority—church, statehouse, magazine [storehouse], office building—all were gutted.[36]

Berkeley was not in the capital at the time. In the face of the rebel army, he had fled to a defensive position near the seashore. Well before the destruction of Jamestown, he had made sure to send word of the rebellion to England, along with a personal appeal to the king for troops and other aid. Berkeley knew that it would take at least one to two months

A Stagnating Frontier

One of the more far-reaching outcomes of the chaotic, sometimes violent period between 1675 and 1720 in the colonies was a significant slowdown in the expansion of the western frontier, as pointed out by historian Thomas L. Purvis.

The English colonial frontier essentially stagnated—and in some areas actually contracted—for more than forty years after 1675 because of the disruption caused by King Philip's War in New England, Bacon's Rebellion in Virginia, the Yamasee and Tuscarora Wars in the Carolinas, and almost uninterrupted warfare against France and its Indian allies from 1689 to 1713. During the four decades af-

ter 1675, the outermost limit of white settlement rarely stretched more than 50 miles from the coastline, except for two thin bands of settlement, one along the Hudson River to Albany, and the other up the Connecticut River to Northampton, Massachusetts. The expansion of the thirteen colonies entered its final phase east of the Appalachians after 1720 when Anglo-Americans began to people the interior counties of New England, New York's Mohawk valley, Pennsylvania's Lancaster plain . . . the Carolina back country, and the thirteenth province of Georgia.

Thomas L. Purvis, *Colonial America to 1763.* New York: Facts On File, 1999, pp. 16, 19.

for help to arrive. In the meantime, he had to deal with the uprising on his own.

Fortunately for the beleaguered governor, two major factors worked to thwart the rebellion. First, a number of Bacon's supporters, who had joined him in the heat of the moment, had second thoughts. Sober reflection told them that sooner or later the king would send soldiers, who would surely round up and hang any rebels they could find. Therefore, large numbers of desertions thinned Bacon's ranks. Then, on October 26, 1676, Bacon suddenly died (probably of dysentery, a digestive disorder that causes severe diarrhea). Without its leader to hold it together, the insurrection quickly fell apart.

Outcomes of the Collective Crises

Having managed, primarily through some fortunate strokes of luck, to emerge the victor in the first American civil war, Berkeley exacted his revenge. His soldiers rooted out twenty-three of Bacon's leading associates and publicly hanged them. The governor also ordered his men to loot and burn the farms of

many lesser rebels. Eventually, the British troops Berkeley had sent for—1,100 of them—arrived, and for the moment, their presence discouraged other would-be insurgents.

Yet Virginia was not the only colony plagued by dissent, rebellion, or other outbreaks of mass violence in this volatile period. Farther south, in the Carolina colony, a similar fight between rival groups of planters—Culpeper's Rebellion—erupted less than a year after Bacon's death. In Maryland in 1689, a farmer named John Coode gathered an army, took the governor prisoner, and occupied the plantation of the powerful Calvert family. In New England, in 1675–1676, twelve towns were destroyed and six hundred settlers were killed in a huge Indian uprising that came to be called King Philip's War. Indian wars nearly as destructive rocked the Carolinas between 1711 and 1717.

Perhaps the most crucial outcome of the colonial crises that began with Bacon's Rebellion was Britain's political takeover of most of the colonies. In the words of one modern scholar:

Royal officials became increasingly concerned about bringing England's overseas empire under stricter control. The quick response to Bacon's Rebellion—the squadron of [1,100] royal troops . . . underscored the crown's deep concern about instability in an area that was becoming an important economic asset. [Thus, the British government] tried to extend its authority in North America. Among other things, royal officials challenged the legality of most of the colonies' charters, which granted liberal terms of self-government.[37]

At the same time, a new social-political order began to emerge in the colonies. The gap between the upper and lower social ranks still existed and in some ways broadened. The big and small farmers who had opposed each other in the rebellions realized that, to survive and prosper, they must work together against outside forces. Over time, these forces became more and more the Indians and the British government, which increasingly imposed its will on the colonies.

Despite sharp social differences among the colonists, together they developed a sense of rivalry toward England, which grew stronger as the 1700s progressed. The colonists still viewed themselves as English, but felt like Americans at the same time, with a unique set of talents and needs. A truly American civilization was beginning to emerge—one that would eventually demand political, as well as cultural, independence.

Chapter Four

THE CHANGING SOCIAL STATUS OF BLACKS

Indentured servants and black slaves always endured low social status and had no political rights in British America. At least the servants could look forward to eventually enjoying their freedom again when their terms of service were over. Most slaves did not have that luxury.

There was an important corollary to this situation, however. Little known today is the fact that the social status and lives of African blacks in the colonies was not always so bleak. In the first few decades of colonial settlement, very few blacks lived in North America. Their status and treatment was very similar, and often identical, to that of white indentured servants. As a result, some blacks gained their freedom, lived alongside free whites, and even fought at the sides of white settlers. For example, evidence shows that a hefty percentage of Nathaniel Bacon's supporters in his bid to seize control of the Virginia Colony were black. More importantly, they were either indentured servants or free farmers, not slaves.

The number of Africans, either slaves or free, in colonial America remained relatively few for a couple of generations. In the late 1600s and early 1700s, however, the number of black slaves in the colonies sharply increased. Partly because they felt threatened by the higher proportion of blacks in society, the white colonists clamped down on them, forcing African Americans into a lower and more subservient status than ever before.

Fellow Sufferers

This tale of the changing social status of colonial blacks begins on a somewhat positive note. Early colonial blacks and white indentured servants worked together

The first African slaves arriving in Jamestown, Virginia, in 1619. In those early days blacks were more commonly referred to as servants rather than as slaves and were seen as equals to white servants.

in the fields, sometimes alongside free white farmers. Members of all three groups put in the same number of hours in an average day or average week. Also, it was customary in early seventeenth-century Virginia for black and white laborers to share the same bunkhouses, eat the same foods, and even to marry and have children together. In those days, most of the few blacks who inhab-ited the colonies were seen by poor whites more as fellow sufferers, rather than as inferiors. Moreover, blacks were more often referred to as servants, or simply as Negroes, than as slaves.

This situation was described fairly vividly by James Revel, a white English convict, who was brought to the colonies in the mid-1600s to work in the fields. There, he regularly worked alongside

African Americans. Later, he fancied himself a poet and described some of his field-working experiences in verses that have survived:

Thus dressed into the field I next must go, amongst tobacco plants all day to hoe. At daybreak in the morn our work began, and so held to the setting of the sun. My fellow slaves were just five transports [white convicts] more, with eighteen Negroes, which is twenty-four [workers altogether]. Besides our transport women [female servants] in the house, to wait upon his [the farm owner's] daughter and his spouse, we and the Negroes both alike did fare, of work and food we had equal share. But in a piece of ground we call our own, the food we eat first by ourselves was grown.[38]

Because these early colonial blacks had a status more like that of indentured servants than slaves, an unknown number of blacks imported into the colonies eventually gained their freedom. Surviving records for Virginia's Northampton County show that in 1668, close to 30 percent of local blacks had gained their freedom. One way this occurred was through deals in which a black servant borrowed money from his owner. With this money, the servant purchased his freedom and, once free, he worked at a job, earned wages, and used some of these wages to pay off the debt. The records also show that a few black servants went so far as to petition the courts to acquire their freedom. The argument they offered was that, like white servants, they had faithfully labored for years on the owner's property. It was only fair that they should be rewarded for their hard work and loyalty by gaining their freedom. A third way that early colonial blacks became free was when they were the products of mixed marriages. When a white man married a female black servant, their mixed-race children were legally free.

Still another aspect of the social status of many early colonial blacks was that they were allowed to own their own land. Again, the records from Northampton County are informative. They indicate that between 1664 and 1677, 13 of that county's 101 black residents owned their own farms. These farmers also owned livestock of various kinds. In addition, some had black servants, and a few even employed white indentured servants. Virginia's legislature did not enact a law banning the use of white servants by black farmers until 1670. Finally, free blacks paid taxes, and in those colonies that allowed it (including New York and Virginia), they voted alongside whites.

Filling the Need for Cheap Labor

This arrangement did not endure, however. One reason was that more and more acres of land in the colonies, especially in the South, came under cultivation. Also, large-scale cash crops, like tobacco, became increasingly prevalent. These factors stimulated the need for a growing number of laborers, and, so that the plantation owners could reap large profits, the more inexpensive these laborers were, the better.

In theory, there were three general approaches to filling this growing need for cheap labor. A plantation owner could use captured Indians as field workers and other kinds of servants. He could send for white indentured servants from England and other parts of Europe. He could also bring in more black Africans to work for him, as the Spanish and Portuguese plantation owners in the Caribbean region did.

Experiments with all of these approaches occurred in the early North American colonies. The first one, enslaving Indians, proved largely unproductive. As John Miller explains, "When enslaved, the natives obstinately refused to work, ran away, or died. Even though the English colonists expended far more effort upon enslaving the Indians than upon converting them to Christianity, it was all to no avail."[39]

White indentured servants were much more efficient as forced laborers than Indians were. The number of these servants greatly decreased over time, however. Florida State University scholar Edward G. Gray tells how this came about:

By the mid-1660s, a falling birthrate and improving economy in England resulted in more jobs for men and women who might otherwise have come to the colonies [as indentured servants]. Similarly, a devastating fire that burned much of London in 1666 created a massive surge in demand for manual labor to rebuild the city. And finally, the rising cost of fertile land in Virginia and Maryland meant diminished opportunities for former servants. Those people still inclined to come to the colonies were now beginning to emigrate to the middle colonies—Pennsylvania, New York, and New Jersey—where land was cheaper.[40]

To make up for this decrease in the number of white servants in the colonies, plantation owners increased their demand for black African, forced workers. The striking change in the proportions of white servants and black workers can be traced in surviving records from York County, in Virginia. The ratio of white to black plantation workers fell from two whites for each black in 1680, to fourteen blacks for each white in 1690, a mere decade apart.

The largest increase in new black laborers in the colonies occurred in Virginia and Maryland. According to Virginia's census records, in 1671 that colony had about 2,000 blacks, making up about 5 percent of the overall population of 40,000. By 1700, however, there were 16,000 blacks in Virginia, constituting more than 30 percent of the population. During these same years, similar increases in the number of colonial black workers took place in every English

Difficult to Enslave Indians

The colonists found it impractical to use Native Americans as slaves and eventually, turned mainly to African blacks. As for the reasons, noted American historian Howard Zinn writes:

[The colonists] were outnumbered and while, with superior firearms, they could massacre Indians, they would face massacre in return. They could not capture them and keep them enslaved [because] the Indians were tough, resourceful, defiant, and at home in the woods, as the transplanted Englishmen were not.

Another respected historian, Edmund Morgan adds:

If you were a colonist, your superior technology had proved insufficient to extract anything. The Indians, keeping to themselves, laughed at your superior methods and lived from the land more abundantly and with less labor than you did. . . . So you killed the Indians, tortured them, burned their villages, burned their cornfields. It proved your superiority, in spite of your failures. . . . But you still did not grow much corn.

Howard Zinn, *A People's History of the United States*. New York: Harper and Row, 2005, p. 25; Edmund S. Morgan, *American Slavery, American Freedom*. New York: Norton, 1975, p. 90.

Virginia colonists capturing a Native American man. The colonists eventually gave up trying to secure Native Americans as slaves because of the difficultly of keeping the natives enslaved.

colony south of Maryland. By contrast, far fewer blacks lived and worked in the northern colonies. In Massachusetts in 1746, for instance, there were only 5,200 African Americans out of a total of about 224,000 residents.

A Society Dependent on Bound Labor

Thus, over time the population of black Africans in the colonies swelled significantly. British America became a society highly dependent overall on bound, or forced, laborers. By the mid-1700s more than 300,000 blacks dwelled in the colonies, making up fully one-fifth of the population. At that point, nearly every person in British America either employed white or black servants, *was* one of these servants, or used products or services provided by such forced laborers. "It is crucial to recognize," Gray writes,

that "bound labor," or servitude and slavery, was much more prevalent in the colonies than in England or the British Isles. Consider [that] as many as half of all Europeans who came to British North America came as in-

Colonial America became highly dependent on slave labor, especially in the southern colonies, where slaves were used on plantations to pick cotton and perform other agricultural tasks.

dentured servants. [Factoring in the large numbers of black slaves brought to the colonies in the colonial era], virtually everyone in the colonies . . . participated in bound or unfree labor systems—systems designed, above all, to transform worthless land into valued property.[41]

The use of both white servants and black slaves was most prevalent in the southern colonies, particularly by well-to-do planters. William Byrd, owner of the famous Westover plantation in Virginia, was completely unapologetic about his forced laborers, writing to a friend in 1726:

Like one of the patriarchs [important men in the Bible], I have my flocks and my herds, my bond-men [slaves] and bond-women, and every sort of trade amongst my own servants, so that I live in a kind of in[ter]dependence on everyone but Providence [God]. However, [this sort of life] is attended by a great deal of trouble. I must take care to keep all my people to their duty, to set all the springs in motion, and to make everyone draw his equal share to carry the machine forward.[42]

Enactment of Slave Laws and Codes

With the number of blacks living and working in the colonies rapidly increasing in the late 1600s and early 1700s,

white society reacted by diminishing blacks' already low social status and minimal civil rights. Africans who arrived in North America could no longer look forward to potentially gaining their freedom. Increasingly, white colonists treated blacks as little more than commodities, rather than fellow human beings, for the duration of their lives. In 1682 Virginia passed a law making black slavery a lifelong institution, and several other colonies did the same in the years that followed.

These were not the only laws passed by white colonists to dominate, control, and reduce the status of African Americans. Before the late 1600s, Virginia had permitted the children of a white father and black mother to be free. But in 1691, the colony's legislature passed a law saying that such children were no longer free. The same year, moreover, it became illegal in Virginia for whites and blacks to intermarry. Any white man who broke this law was banished from the colony thereafter. Other laws in Virginia and elsewhere disallowed blacks from carrying weapons, leaving the owner's property without his or her permission, owning property, going out at night without permission from a white person, and challenging white authority in any way.

Soon, individual laws pertaining to slaves that had been passed intermittently were replaced by more comprehensive collections of statutes that came to be called "slave codes" or "black codes." The first sweeping slave code was

Baptized Slaves are Still Slaves

In 1668 the Virginia legislature passed a law saying that Christian baptism was not a route to freedom for blacks. The text of the law reads:

Whereas some doubts have risen whether children that are slaves by birth and by the charity and piety of their owners made partakers of the Blessed Sacrament of Baptism should by virtue of their baptism be made free. It is enacted and declared by the Grand assembly and the authority thereof that the conferring of baptism does not alter the conditions of the person as to his bondage or freedom; that diverse masters freed from this doubt may more carefully endeavor the propagation of Christianity by permitting children, though slaves, or those of greater growth if capable, to be admitted to that Sacrament.

Quoted in Edward G. Gray, *Colonial America: A History in Documents.* New York: Oxford University Press, 2003, p. 97.

---

enacted in South Carolina in 1696. Titled the *Act for the Better Ordering and Governing of Negroes and Slaves,* its preface stated in part:

Whereas, the plantations and estates of this province cannot be well and sufficiently managed and brought into use without the labor and service of Negroes and other slaves [a reference to Indians]; and [because] the said Negroes and other slaves brought into . . . this province for that purpose are of barbarous, wild, savage natures, and such as renders them wholly unqualified to be governed by the laws, customs, and practices of this province [we declare that] it is absolutely necessary that such [laws] and [rules] be made and enacted for the good of regulating and [controlling said slaves].[43]

Since the black slaves were "barbarous and savage," the reasoning concluded that they were less than human. Because the ordinary laws pertaining to physical abuse and murder were designed for human beings, they did not apply to African Americans. In this way, white owners and overseers justified treating their slaves in any manner they saw fit. It is true that a few whites did continue to treat their black slaves the same way they did their white servants—firmly but humanely. But a majority resorted to methods that today would be seen as abusive. Some slave owners outright raped, mutilated, and murdered their slaves at will.

Moreover, white society made sure to protect the more abusive characters in their ranks. In 1705 Virginia enacted a law that said there would be no punishment whatsoever for a slave owner who killed a slave while disciplining him or her. Similar statutes were passed in most of the colonies. Conversely, these same colonies made laws that made the crime of a slave killing a white person punishable by execution.

The Lowest Rung on the Ladder

The increasing dehumanization of colonial blacks, along with the creation of harsh, inhumane laws to control them, steadily reduced their social status to the lowest rung on the social ladder. The speed at which this process worked varied from colony to colony. Slavery was not even legal in some colonies at first, including Pennsylvania, Rhode Island, Connecticut, and Maryland. Connecticut made it legal in 1650, Maryland in 1663, Pennsylvania in 1700, and Rhode Island in 1715. By the 1720s the process of dehumanizing African Americans and reducing their social status to near insignificance was complete.

Occupying the bottom of the social ladder left colonial black Americans open not only to abuses by their owners, but also to mistreatment on a wider, societal level. In other words, black slavery became institutionalized. With this broad transformation of the social structure came changes in the way people of all social classes thought about blacks. In the colonies' early decades, the issue of their race had been secondary to their legal rights as working servants. Now, they were no longer merely unfortunate fellow sufferers along with the white servants. Instead, the fact of their race had become inseparable from their low social status. In this way, overt antiblack racism became institutionalized in American society along with low black social status, all within only two or three generations.

A poster offering a reward for a runaway slave. Advertisements like this were especially common in the southern colonies, where the economy relied on slave labor.

Stop the Runaway!

$100 Reward!

Ranaway from the subscriber, living in Clay county, Mo., 3 miles south of Haynesville and 15 miles north of Liberty, a negro boy named SANDY, about 35 years of age, about 5 feet 6 inches high, rather copper color, whiskers in his chin, quick when spoken to, had on when he left brown janes pants and coat, black plush cap, and coarse boots. If apprehended a reward of $25 will be given if taken in Clay county; $50 if out of the county, and $100 if taken out of the State, and delivered to me or confined in jail so that I can get him.   ROBT. THOMPSON.
April 3, 1860.

A great deal of evidence of this institutionalized racism has survived. For example, written depictions of blacks as subhuman or as mere property were common in colonial newspapers and posters. An ad in the June 6, 1763, issue of Rhode Island's *Newport Gazette* described some newly arrived Africans this way:

> On Thursday last arrived from the coast of Africa, the brig *Royal Charlotte* with a parcel of extremely fine, healthy, well-limbed Gold Coast slaves—men, women, boys, and girls. Gentlemen in town and country have now an opportunity to furnish themselves with such [slaves] as will suit them. [The slaves] are to be seen [and inspected] on the vessel at Taylor's wharf.[44]

Ads for runaway slaves also were common, especially in the southern colonies. These often provided detailed descriptions of the runaways, to better ensure they would be recognized and captured. (Such ads tell modern historians much about the appearance and experiences of colonial blacks.) Because these descriptions resembled those used in selling cattle and other livestock, they also perpetuated the dehumanization of blacks. The following example is from the June 15, 1739, issue of the *Virginia Gazette:*

Two Slaves in a Canoe

Surviving newspaper and poster ads for runaway slaves have proven to be valuable in revealing how colonial whites viewed blacks and exemplifying a number of social aspects of blacks, including their modes of dress. This example was printed in the Virginia Gazette *on May 9, 1745:*

R an away . . . from the Plantation of the late Col. William Wilson, deceas'd, Two Slaves belonging to the subscriber [Mary Wilson], the one a tall yellow Fellow, named Emanuel, about 6 Feet high, six or seven and Twenty Years of Age; [he] hath a scar on the outside of his left Thigh, which was cut with an Ax; he had on when he went away, a blue Jacket . . . he speaks pretty good English. . . . The other [runaway] is a short, thick, well-set Fellow [who] stoops forward pretty much as he walks; [he] does not speak so plain as the other; [he] had on when he went away . . . [a] Pair of Trousers and [a] Shirt, a white Negro Cotton Jacket, and took with him an Axe: They went away in a small Cannoe.

Quoted in Lathan A. Windley, *Runaway Slave Advertisements: A Documentary History from the 1730s to 1790,* Vol. 1. Westport, CT: Greenwood, 1983, p. 12.

Ran away from the subscriber [the owner, William Drummond], on Sunday the 17th . . . a pale complexioned mulatto [mixed race] fellow named Natt, with straw hair about 2 or 3 inches long. He is a thick, well-set fellow, about 26 years old, has several black moles on his face, a full mouth, black teeth, small forehead, and broad feet. . . . He had on an old hat, cotton waistcoat, and patched breeches [pants] and a [heavy linen] shirt. . . . Whoever will bring the said mulatto slave to me . . . shall receive a [special] reward, besides what the law allows.[45]

Views of this sort seem particularly jarring and pitiless today. After all, American blacks are accepted members of society, so much so that the United States elected its first African American president in 2008. Such ads also are educational. For example, they show that, although colonial society and modern society were alike in some ways, in others they were strikingly, and in this case disturbingly, different.

Chapter Five

THE IMPACT OF THE ENLIGHTENMENT

Had the politics and society of British America continued to operate indefinitely as they did in 1700, the history of the world would undoubtedly have been quite different. The reality, though, was that they changed significantly. One of the main engines of that change was a seventeenth- and eighteenth-century intellectual movement usually referred to as the European Enlightenment. Led initially by liberal English and French thinkers, it steadily spread to England's North American colonies, where numerous colonial leaders absorbed its basic doctrines and ideas over time. These ideas transformed theories of government in these colonies and ultimately spearheaded the American Revolution.

The Enlightenment marked one of the most crucial changes in human thought in history. Compared to the widespread intolerance, brutality, and "might makes right" mentality of past ages, its concepts were enlightened or open minded, progressive, and humane. Among these concepts was a recognition that the world worked by scientific principles. Others included religious toleration and the existence of certain basic natural human rights. Washington State University scholar Richard Hooker lists some of the other major ideas contained in Enlightenment thinking and writing:

The universe is fundamentally rational, that is, it can be understood through the use of reason alone; truth can be arrived at through empirical [practical] observation, the use of reason, and systematic doubt; human experience is the foundation of human understanding of truth; authority is not to be preferred over experience; all human life, both social and individual, can be understood in the same way the natural world can be understood; once understood, human life, both social and individual, can be manipulated or engineered in the same way the natural world can be manipulated or engineered; human history is largely a history of progress; human beings can be improved through education and the development of their rational [faculties].[46]

Roots in Natural Law

Enlightenment thinkers, especially in the American colonies, came to believe that humans could remake society and government, making both more equitable and just. The basis for this thinking did not consist simply in a few bright, well-intentioned individuals suddenly concluding that life should be more fair. Rather, the movement was largely based on the notion that certain basic natural laws existed. These laws ultimately favored the right of freedom of thought and self-expression. They could be revealed through careful, patient studies of the natural world. During the Enlightenment, Alan Taylor points out:

Educated Europeans assumed that the universe of both mind and matter obeyed predictable natural laws, rather than arbitrary [random] dictates of an inscrutable [unknowable] God. Rejecting ancient texts as a sufficient proof, enlightened Europeans sought more systematically to collect and organize new information about everything on Earth (and beyond). . . . In publications circulating through the learned circles of the European elite, new discoveries became a medium for the competitive pursuit of national prestige.[47]

Although they finally found wide expression in the Enlightenment, such ideas about natural law were not new. Some two thousand years before, a number of Greek and Roman thinkers had discussed such concepts. Aristotle, a fourth-century B.C. Greek scholar, wrote extensively about the idea of justice, for instance. There is the familiar legal kind of justice, he said, involving courts and juries. But there is also a natural sort of justice that belongs to all people in all nations. In a similar manner, a first-century B.C. Roman senator, Cicero, argued that this more universal kind of law quietly exists in human hearts and minds, inspiring people to try to do right and just things (even if they do not always succeed). This special brand of law is the naturally occurring power of reason, he declared.

It is spread through the whole human community, unchanging and eternal, calling people to their duty by its commands and deterring them from wrong-doing by its prohibitions. . . . The law [of nature] cannot be countermanded, nor can it be totally . . . rescinded. There will not be one such law in Rome and another in Athens, one now and another in the future, but all peoples in all times will be embraced by a single and eternal and unchangeable [natural] law.[48]

Enlightenment thinkers and writers, both in Europe and colonial America, were aware of and admired these ancient ideas about natural law. Their great contribution was to reinterpret these concepts

The ideas expressed by the Enlightenment thinkers in the American colonies were not new and were actually expressed in the first century B.C. by the Roman senator Cicero, pictured here.

and attempt to apply them to theories about human rights and the structure and conduct of government. This reexamination and new application of such ideas steadily and profoundly changed the way a number of educated European and Americans viewed their political and social institutions.

Locke and the Right to Liberty

One of the strongest of these intellectual voices that helped to transform American politics and society was the seventeenth-century English writer John Locke (1632–1704). He believed that traditional societies governed by kings and other absolute rulers almost always suppressed the basic human rights inherent in natural law. His classic work *Two Treatises of Government* (1690) stated that politics and government should not be subject to the arbitrary personal whims of a king or queen. Rather, any sound government should be shaped by and subject to the will of those who are governed. Moreover, a government's chief duty should be to protect the natural rights, including life, liberty, and property, of its citizens. He argued:

> To understand political power, we must consider what state all men are naturally in, and that is a state of perfect freedom to order their actions and dispose of their possessions [as] they think fit, within the bounds of the law of nature, with-

out asking leave or depending upon the will of any other man.

Going hand and hand with "perfect freedom," Locke said, is a "state of equality," which he defined as one in which "all the power and jurisdiction is reciprocal [shared by all], no one having more than another."[49]

Locke also emphasized that no person, whether inside or outside of government, has the right to deny fellow citizens their rights to life, liberty, or personal property. The natural law of reason, he stated,

> teaches all mankind . . . that, being equal and independent, no one ought to harm another in his life, health, liberty, or possessions. . . . And that all men may be restrained from invading others' rights and from doing hurt to one another, and the law of nature be observed, which wills the peace and preservation of all mankind, the execution of the law of nature is, in that state, put into every man's hands. . . . In transgressing the law of nature, the offender declares himself to live by another rule than that of reason and common equity; which is that measure God has set to the actions of men for their mutual security.[50]

These concepts, of course, were eventually adopted by colonial thinkers and leaders, including Thomas Jefferson and other U.S. founding fathers. Another important concept of Locke's they borrowed was the notion that when a ruler tramples on the rights of the citizens they are justified in rising up against that ruler. "The end of government is the good of mankind," Locke wrote. "And which is best for mankind? That the people should be always exposed to the boundless will of tyranny, or that the rulers should be sometimes liable to be opposed when they grow exorbitant [excessive] in the use of their power and employ it for the destruction and not the preservation of the properties of their people?"[51]

It is important to emphasize that the ideas of Locke and other Enlightenment thinkers did not suddenly begin making an impact on colonial political thought in Jefferson's era (late colonial times). Instead, these ideas began circulating in the colonies long before. Educated colonists read Locke's books well before Jefferson was born, and colonial clergymen regularly used Locke's political and moral concepts in their sermons. As a result, over time these ideas became ingrained in the thinking of many colonists. By the time Jefferson was an adult, many colonial politicians did not simply try to copy Locke, but rather had already learned to think and write like him.

Other Enlightened Political Ideas

This same pattern of colonial exposure to, and then steady absorption of, political ideas happened with other European Enlightenment thinkers besides

Locke. Educated colonists also were exposed to and influenced by the great French political philosopher, historian, and jurist, Charles de Montesquieu (1689–1755); English philosopher and essayist Francis Bacon (1561–1626); English mathematician and natural philosopher Isaac Newton (1642–1727); English/Scottish philosopher Francis Hutcheson (1694–1746); English political theorist Algernon Sidney (1622–1683); and the French philosophers Voltaire (François Marie Arouet, 1694–1778), and Jean-Jacques Rousseau (1712–1778).

The case of Sidney, who lived and worked during the initial founding and development of England's North American colonies, shows how such ideas crossed the Atlantic and found fertile soil to grow in.

Sidney, whose most famous work was *Discourses Concerning Government,* was considered a radical, even dangerous, thinker in seventeenth-century England. This was because he, like Locke, believed that citizens should be able to rid themselves of a corrupt or repressive government. Sidney advocated that revolution was a perfectly acceptable way to do this. "To Sidney," scholar Murray N. Rothbard explains,

> revolution and freedom were closely linked. Whenever people's liberties were threatened or invaded, they had the right, nay the *duty,* to rebel. . . . Revolution to Sidney was not an evil but the people's great weapon for the overthrow of tyranny and for exercising their rights to popular government. There was nothing sacred about governments, which on the contrary should be changed as required. The types of law necessary in a country were to be discerned by man's reason investigating the fundamental laws of man's nature. Against the arbitrary whim of the ruler, Sidney championed law as "written reason" and as defense of life, liberty, and property. . . . Power, he warned, inevitably corrupts and every institutional power must be guarded against. To Sidney, government rested on a contract between government and governed. When government fails to perform its role in the service of the people, it deserves to be removed.[52]

Sidney's ideas about government and the rights of citizens spread rapidly through the early American colonies. Noted Boston Congregational ministers Andrew Eliot and Jonathan Mayhew (who coined the phrase "no taxation without representation") were strongly influenced by them. They, and many other colonial Americans, found such ideas not subversive or dangerous, but enlightening and inspiring. As happened with Locke's ideas, Sidney's ideas took hold and increased in popularity during the American Revolution.

A similar scenario transpired with some of Montesquieu's concepts of effective and just politics and government. Like other

Algerenon Sydney

Bn. 1622

Quo fata vocant

Seventeenth-century political theorist Algernon Sidney was considered a radical, and even dangerous, thinker because he believed that citizens should be able to rid themselves of a corrupt or repressive government.

Reinventing Natural Law

The thinkers and writers who created the European Enlightenment in the 1600s and 1700s did not invent all of their ideas about natural law and natural human rights. Rather, they reinvented and built on a number of concepts that had been introduced thousands of years before by Greek and Roman thinkers. For example, the fourth-century B.C. Greek scholar Aristotle discussed the idea of "natural" justice in his Ethics. *"There are two sorts of political justice," he said,*

One natural and the other legal. The natural is that which has the same validity everywhere and does not depend upon acceptance [in any specific place or time]; the legal is that which . . . once laid down, is decisive, [for example] that . . . a goat shall be sacrificed and not two sheep. . . . Some hold the view that all regulations are of this kind, on the grounds that whereas natural laws are immutable [unchangeable] and have the same validity everywhere (as fire burns both here and in Persia), they can see the notions of justice are variable . . . but still, some things are so by nature and some are not.

Aristotle, *Ethics*, published as *The Ethics of Aristotle*. Trans. J.A.K. Thomson, rev. Hugh Tredennick. New York: Penguin, 1976, pp. 189–190.

Enlightenment thinkers, Montesquieu was against political tyranny, which he warned was likely to occur when too much power rested in the hands of only a few individuals. In shaping or reshaping government, therefore, the people should separate the various governmental branches and give some power to each. That way, it will be harder for one branch to dominate the entire government. In his highly influential 1748 treatise *The Spirit of the Laws*, he called for dividing government into legislative, executive, and judicial branches and said:

When legislative power is united with executive power in a single person or in a single body . . . there is no liberty, because one can fear that the same monarch or senate that makes tyrannical laws will execute them tyrannically. Nor is there liberty if the power of judging is not separate from legislative power and from executive power. If it were joined to legislative power, the power over the life and liberty of the citizens would be arbitrary [subject to the whims of the powerful]. If it were joined to executive power, the judge could have the force of an oppressor. All would be lost if the same man or the same body of principal men . . . exercised these three powers, that of making laws, that of executing public resolutions, and that of judging the crimes or the disputes of individuals.[53]

These ideas became so ingrained in the thinking of late colonial leaders that they readily incorporated them into the governmental blueprint of the infant United States.

Influences of American Thinkers

Not all of the new political ideas that steadily took hold in the colonies came from English, French, and other European thinkers and writers. Most colonial American political and religious leaders were highly educated individuals. Some not only felt the influence of European thought, but also made contributions to the Enlightenment themselves.

Among the most prominent of these individuals was Benjamin Franklin (1706–1790). His career, like those of some other colonial thinkers and inventors, demonstrated how the colonists could absorb new ideas from across the ocean and then create ideas of their own that would eventually cross back over and influence Europeans. As one expert observer notes:

Like other Americans who imbibed [absorbed] the "new learning," [Franklin] was most impressed by its emphasis on useful knowledge and experimentation. He pondered air currents and then invented a stove

that heated houses more efficiently. He toyed with electricity and then invented lightning rods to protect buildings in thunderstorms. Other amateur American scientists also hoped to understand and master the natural world. They constructed simple telescopes to observe the tran-

The influence of the Enlightenment thinkers can be found in Thomas Jefferson's writings, including The Declaration of Independence.

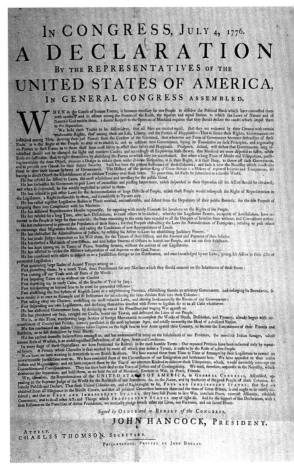

sits of Venus and Mercury [across the sun's disk]; they filled botanical gardens with plants and identified and classified animal species native to North America. They sought to explain epidemics in terms of natural causes, [and] experimented with new farming techniques and wrote trea-

tises on increasing the productivity of agriculture.[54]

A younger colonial contemporary of Franklin's, Thomas Jefferson (1743–1826), also was both a product and innovator of the Enlightenment. Born in Virginia, Jefferson was well educated and as a young man read the works of Bacon, Newton, Sidney, Locke, and other members of the European Enlightenment. He went on to write some of the greatest democratic political documents of all time. These included *A Summary View of the Rights of British America, The Virginia Statute for Religious Freedom,* and *The Declaration of Independence.* The influence of Locke and the others plainly can be seen in these works. By no means, however, did Jefferson merely repeat their ideas and words. Rather, he selected and reinterpreted portions of them, and then in his own writings, went beyond them to make bold and, at the time, radical statements about political liberties.

Virginia's Declaration of Rights, *written by George Mason, emphasized the idea that people's happiness was a political right akin to free speech and freedom of religion.*

VIRGINIA BILL *of* RIGHTS

DRAWN ORIGINALLY BY GEORGE MASON AND
ADOPTED BY THE CONVENTION OF DELEGATES

June 12, 1776.

A Declaration of Rights made by the Representatives of the good People of Virginia, assembled in full and free Convention; which Rights do pertain to them, and their Posterity, as the Basis and Foundation of Government.

I.

That all Men are by Nature equally free and independent, and have certain inherent Rights, of which, when they enter into a State of Society, they cannot, by any Compact, deprive or divest their Posterity; namely, the Enjoyment of Life and Liberty, with the Means of acquiring and possessing Property, and pursuing and obtaining Happiness and Safety.

II.

That all Power is vested in, and consequently derived from, the People; that Magistrates are their Trustees and Servants, and at all Times amenable to them.

III.

That Government is, or ought to be, instituted for the common Benefit, Protection, and Security, of the People, Nation, or Community; of all the various Modes and Forms of Government that is best, which is capable of producing the greatest Degree of Happiness and Safety, and is most effectually secured against the Danger of Mal-administration; and that, whenever any Government shall be found inadequate or contrary to these Purposes, a Majority of the Community hath an indubitable, unalienable, and indefeasible Right, to reform, alter, or abolish it, in such Manner as shall be judged most conducive to the public Weal.

IV.

That no Man, or Set of Men, are entitled to exclusive or separate Emoluments or Privileges from the Community, but in Consideration of public Services; which, not being descendible, neither ought the Offices of Magistrate, Legislator, or Judge, to be hereditary.

V.

That the legislative and executive Powers of the State should be separate and distinct from the Judicative; and, that the Members of the two first may be restrained from Oppression, by feeling and participating the Burthens of the People, they should, at fixed Periods, be reduced into a private Station, return into that Body from which they were originally taken, and the Vacancies be supplied by frequent, certain, and regular Elections, in which all, or any Part of the former Members, to be again eligible, or ineligible, as the Laws shall direct.

That

A New View of Human Happiness

A striking example of the unique ways that colonial Americans like Jefferson reinterpreted Enlightenment ideas was an essentially new way of viewing human happiness. Liberal European thinkers had sometimes listed the contentment of the citizenry as one of the many goals of good government. Political and social writers in the colonies readily embraced this concept.

The Gospel of Progress

One of the leading voices of the Enlightenment was French thinker and mathematician Nicolas de Condorcet (1743–1794). More than any other enlightened concept, he championed the idea of progress, saying it was a moral absolute that would eventually liberate people everywhere from poverty, ignorance, war, gender inequality, and tyranny. In his unfinished masterpiece, The Progress of the Human Mind, *he wrote:*

French thinker and mathematician Nicolas de Condorcet was a leading voice of the Enlightenment and a champion of the idea of progress.

Among the causes of the progress of the human mind that are of the utmost importance to the general happiness, we must number the complete annihilation of the prejudices that have brought about an inequality of rights between the sexes, an inequality fatal even to the party in whose favor it works [i.e., men]. [The] inequality [between men and women] has its origin solely in an abuse of strength, and all the later [philosophical] attempts that have been made to excuse it are in vain. . . . Once people are enlightened, they will know that they have the right to dispose of their own life and wealth as they choose. They will gradually learn to regard war as the most dreadful of scourges, the most terrible of crimes, [and] nations will learn that they cannot conquer other nations without losing their own liberty.

Nicolas de Condorcet, *The Progress of the Human Mind*, excerpted in Charles Hirschfeld and Edgar E. Knoebel, eds., *Classics of Western Thought: The Modern World*. New York: Harcourt Brace Jovanovich, 1980, pp. 253–254.

How New Ideas Spread in the Colonies

In colonial America, the ideas of the Enlightenment spread by many means, including the importation of books from Europe, college courses, and clergymen's pulpits. By 1763 there were six notable colleges in the colonies: Harvard in Massachusetts, William and Mary in Virginia, Yale in Connecticut, the College of New Jersey (later Princeton), King's College (later Columbia) in New York, and the Academy and College of Philadelphia (later the University of Pennsylvania). In addition to courses on religion, these institutions taught mathematics, science, and other subjects in which the latest Enlightenment ideas were discussed. Also, by 1740 many Protestant ministers had begun to preach a more liberal brand of theology than the stricter versions that had existed when the colonies were founded. This so-called "rational Christianity" pictured God less a vengeful, grim character out to punish sinners and more as a benevolent, forgiving one who wanted to see humans be productive and happy. These clergymen stressed doing good works and promoted Enlightenment ideas about human rights as a partial means to achieve a fair, equitable, and happy society.

Still, they went further and began speaking of people's happiness as a full-fledged political right akin to free speech and freedom of religion. Jefferson's colleague, George Mason (1725–1792), one of the so-called fathers of the U.S. Bill of Rights, emphasized this right in Virginia's *Declaration of Rights,* which he wrote in 1776. Other prominent colonial Americans mentioned it as well, among them John Adams, Thomas Paine, George Washington, and, most famously, Jefferson himself, in *The Declaration of Independence.*

What exactly did American thinkers, writers, and leaders mean by happiness in the political sense? Europeans like Locke defined happiness rather loosely, as enjoying a safe, comfortable life. By tradition in Europe, this was largely a privilege of the socially well born and well-to-do. Colonial American thinkers, in contrast, came to view happiness more as the birthright of all citizens, no matter what their wealth and social rank. In the words of noted American historian Henry S. Commager, in Europe happiness was basically an elitist concept affecting a privileged few, whereas:

America had no elite—not, certainly in the Old World sense of the term. Happiness here was presumed to be available to all who were white, and it consisted not in the enjoyment of art and literature, science and philosophy, and social position, but rather in material comfort, freedom, independence, and access to opportunity. Happiness meant milk for the children, and meat on the table, and a well-built house. . . [and] freedom from tyranny of the state, the superstition of the church, [and] the authority of the military.[55]

Therefore, in retrospect, the colonial American branch of the Enlightenment achieved something momentous. American thinkers took the best liberal, progressive ideas of European thinkers and applied them to the political realities of British America. In so doing, they created what was, in effect, a new and innately modern and enlightened civilization.

Chapter Six

GROWING DISPUTES WITH THE MOTHER COUNTRY

About 169 years elapsed between the founding of England's first North American colony at Jamestown in 1607 and the start of the American Revolution in 1775–1776. The entire development and social and political history of British colonial America occurred during those seventeen decades. Looking back, one is struck by the fact that, while colonial society was always changing and evolving, one aspect of politics and government remained steadfast and firm through nearly that entire period. Namely, all colonists saw themselves as British subjects, or Britons. They were not only loyal to the mother country, but also proud to represent it and its growing empire.

Only in the very last of the seventeen decades did major political disputes with the British government arise in the colonies. Moreover, only in the last year or two of the entire colonial period did the colonies seriously consider the idea of separating from Britain to create their own nation. Indeed, very little separatist feeling existed in the colonies before 1775, Samuel Morison points out. Prior to that, he says, the colonists did not feel "that they were so downtrodden by tyrannical masters as to make independence the only solution. On the contrary, Americans were not only content but proud to be part of the British imperium [empire]. But they did feel very strongly that they were entitled to all constitutional rights that Englishmen possessed in England."[56]

Morison's last statement contains the key to why British colonial politics and society eventually morphed into independent American politics and society. As long as they felt the mother country recognized their rights as Britons, the colonists gave no thought to independence. In the 1760s, however, British leaders unwisely initiated policies that seemed to threaten those cherished rights. The disputes that erupted over these policies marked the last traces of colonial politics and government.

Joy and Pride in Victory

The degree to which colonial politics stayed tied to British politics and the colonists long remained loyal Britons can be seen by colonial reactions to the French and Indian War. Actually, this was the North American theater of a larger conflict known as the Seven Years War, which was centered in Europe. Lasting from 1754 to 1763, it pitted Britain and Prussia (now Germany) against a coalition consisting of Austria, France, Russia, Sweden, and other states. On North American soil, they fought to decide who would control colonization there in the future. Britain and France were the principal opponents.

Britain eventually won the French and Indian War. As the victor, it gained extensive territories, including southern Canada and the lands lying between the original thirteen colonies and the Mississippi River. The victory occurred mainly because Britain was better at sending and supporting large armies overseas than was France. "The British overwhelmed [most of the French colonies] with sheer numbers of soldiers and sailors, warships, and cannons," Alan Taylor says.

Two maps showing how the American colonies were divided before (top) and after (below) the French and Indian War.

BEFORE THE FRENCH AND INDIAN WAR.

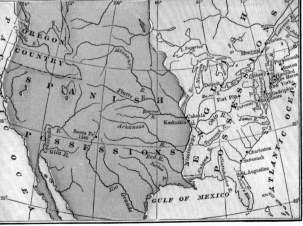

AFTER THE FRENCH AND INDIAN WAR.

Growing Disputes with the Mother Country   73

The ability to project military power across the Atlantic reflected British superiority in shipping, finance, and organization. And that superiority reflected the more advanced nature of Britain as a capitalist society. . . . The British had more money, spent it with wild abandon, and concentrated their expenditures in North America. . . . The conquest of Canada cost the British Empire about 4 million [pounds], more than ten times what the French spent to defend it. Never before had an empire spent so much money to wage war on a transoceanic scale.[57]

The British victory filled the local colonists, who had helped in the war effort, with joy and pride. There were celebrations across the colonies, and many towns raised statues of Britain's king George III. A Massachusetts clergyman, Thomas Barnard, captured the feelings of a majority of colonists when he said:

Now commences the era of our quiet enjoyment of those liberties which our fathers purchased with the toil of their whole lives, their treasure, their blood. Safe from the enemy of the wilderness, safe from the gripping hand of arbitrary sway [rule] and cruel superstition. Here shall be the late founded seat of peace and freedom. Here shall our indulgent mother [country], who has most generously rescued and protected us, be served and honored by growing numbers, with all duty, love, and gratitude, till time shall be no more.[58]

Deciding to Tax the Colonies

The colonists soon found themselves caught up in a difficult financial situation stemming from the war and their defeat by Britain. The mother country had not only spent enormous amounts of money waging the war, but also now faced the reality that maintaining control over its huge American possessions was going to be almost as costly. In particular, military leaders insisted that the wartime troop strength of eighty-five regiments—about nine thousand men—be maintained indefinitely. Paying for these troops, many of whom had to be stationed overseas, was extremely expensive.

One way that British leaders tried to solve this problem was to raise extra money by taxing the American colonists. The first post-war tax of this kind was the American Revenue Act of 1764. It covered a number of important products the colonists imported on a regular basis, including sugar, silk, wine, and linen. Some colonial assemblies made it clear that they did not like the new tax scheme. New York, for example, sent a petition to King George III and Parliament saying that their colony should be exempt from any tax not imposed by its own legislators. In North Carolina, the assembly complained to the royal governor about "new taxes and impositions

Angry at being taxed without representation in Parliament, Stamp Act protesters burn stamps in New York City.

laid on us without our privy and consent, and against what we esteem our inherent right, and exclusive privilege of imposing our own taxes."[59]

The level of colonial discontent raised by the 1764 tax paled in comparison to the one that accompanied a new set of taxes imposed in the following year. Collectively referred to as the Stamp Act, they were levied on paper, parchment, and other products people used for writing and printing. Newspapers, pamphlets, business documents, court papers, playing cards, and many other important items were affected. The new act set up an American Stamp Office in London and installed one stamp distributor for each of nine districts in the colonies.

Colonial reactions to the Stamp Act were loud and sometimes even violent. Angry citizens denounced, and at times physically assaulted, the tax collectors and other Stamp Act officers. In New York, a mob ransacked one such officer's house, and in Boston, furious citizens hanged the local stamp officer in effigy and destroyed his shop. Afterward, they attacked the homes of royal tax collectors, burning their furniture and tossing their books and personal effects into the streets. At the same time, colonial assemblies lodged official protests. Virginia's House of Burgesses stated adamantly:

The General Assembly of this colony has the only and sole exclusive right and power to lay taxes and impositions upon the inhabitants of this colony, and . . . every attempt to vest

such power in any persons whatsoever other than the general assembly aforesaid has a manifest tendency to destroy British as well as American freedom.[60]

Fair Representation Versus Obedience

The argument that the colonists should not be taxed by Parliament without having representatives in that body was not peculiar to British America. Rather, it was a fundamental tenet of English rights going back many generations. For that reason, some members of Parliament opposed the Stamp Act and expressed sympathy with the colonial protests, or at least the nonviolent ones. They and the protesters echoed the view expressed by Benjamin Franklin, when, on a trip to England, some members of the Commons questioned him on the matter. He told them that the colonists

are entitled to all the privileges and liberties of Englishmen; they find in the great charters, and the petition and declaration of rights [parts of the English Constitution], that one of the privileges of English subjects is that they are not to be taxed but by their common consent. They have therefore relied upon it, from the first settlement of the province, that the Parliament never would, never could . . . assume a right of taxing them, till it had qualified itself to exercise such right by admitting representatives [to Parliament] from the people to be taxed.[61]

The majority of British legislators and citizens who supported the Stamp Act were not convinced by Franklin's argument. They simply did not understand the opposition, an opinion concisely expressed by George Grenville, the British prime minister who had spearheaded the Stamp Act bill. "Great Britain protects America," he said, and

America is bound to yield obedience. If not, tell me when the Americans were emancipated? When they want the protection of this kingdom, they are always very ready to ask it. That protection has always been afforded them in the most full and ample manner. The nation has run itself into an immense debt to give them this protection; and now they are called upon to contribute a small share towards the public expense.[62]

Grenville's comments show just how far apart British politics and colonial politics had grown in the space of only a century and a half. He and his supporters viewed the colonies more as overseas possessions than as part of Britain itself. As such, he expected the colonists to be grateful for whatever aid the mother country was willing to provide, including protection from European powers trying to take over North America. For their parts, the colonists had firmly come to see themselves as British citizens with

"Taxation and Representation Are Inseparable"

In the 1760s and 1770s, a number of British leaders, both inside and outside of Parliament, agreed with colonial arguments that stressed the notion of no taxation without representation. One, who spoke out, was the highly respected Lord Camden, who told the House of Lords in 1766:

Taxation and representation are inseparable; this position is founded on the laws of nature. It is more. It is itself an external law of nature; for whatever is a man's own, is absolutely his own. No man has a right to take it from him without his consent, either expressed by himself or [a] representative; whoever attempts to do it, attempts an injury; whoever does it commits a robbery; he throws down and destroys the distinction between liberty and slavery.

Lord Camden, "Speech to House of Lords on American Taxation, February 24, 1766," in Max Beloff, ed., *The Debate on the American Revolution, 1761–1783*. London: Adam and Charles Black, 1960, p. 121.

all of the same rights of Britons living inside England's borders.

Still Another Tax Scheme

Eventually giving in to colonial demands, in March 1766 Parliament repealed the Stamp Act. As had happened after the British victory in the French and Indian War, celebrations took place in every colony. Many colonists who had vigorously protested against the Stamp Act now expressed renewed feelings of loyalty to Britain. They assumed that the tax's repeal was a sign that British leaders were going to treat the colonies fairly after all.

This positive assumption proved premature, however. Britain still desperately needed money to maintain its soldiers in North America. So, in 1767 Parliament passed still another tax scheme, which became known as the Townshend Acts. These taxes affected goods the colonies imported directly from Britain, including lead, paints, paper, and tea.

Reactions in the colonies were once again loud and angry. The prevailing attitude was summed up by Philadelphia lawyer John Dickinson. In his twelve *Farmer's Letters* published in colonial newspapers late in 1767, he called the Townshend taxes every bit as unfair and

Remaining Britons Until the Last Minute

The idea of separating from the mother country did not become inevitable to colonial leaders until the proverbial last minute. Even after the initial blood had been shed in the colonies in 1775, most of these men, including George Washington, Thomas Jefferson, and John Jay, hoped to reconcile with Britain. They wanted Parliament to repeal the Coercive Acts, to stop trying to tax the colonies, and to act more reasonably, in general. At one point, colonial leaders considered a plan that would have kept the bonds between the colonies and mother country intact, but would have revised their existing relationship.

Called the Plan of Union, it was introduced by Pennsylvania's Joseph Galloway. He suggested creating an American version of Parliament, a legislative body that would have veto powers over the British Parliament in matters regarding the American colonies. The new colonial government, Galloway proposed, would be run by a "President-General" whom the British king would appoint and a "Grand Council" whose members would be colonists elected by their peers. The Plan of Union soon fell by the wayside, and as larger events overshadowed it, the colonists chose to start their own country instead.

objectionable as the Stamp Act. "We cannot be happy without being free," he said. And further:

> We cannot be free without being secure in our property—that we cannot be secure in our property if without our consent others may . . . take it away—that taxes imposed on us by Parliament do thus take it away—that duties [taxes] raised for the sole purpose of raising money are taxes—that attempts to lay such duties should be instantly and firmly opposed—that this opposition can never be effectual unless it is the united effort of these provinces.[63]

The "united effort" Dickinson called for materialized as colonial merchants boycotted the British goods covered under the Townshend Acts. To make up for the boycotted goods, citizens of all social ranks became involved in home industries, including making their own clothes and growing their own tea, rather than buying these items from Britain. This approach was successful. Demand for imports from Britain fell by almost a third, forcing Parliament to repeal the Townshend Acts in 1770.

The Tea Party and the Tavern

A lone exception to this repeal was the tax on imported tea, which the British stubbornly kept in force. Few colonists engaged in political protests against the tax, however, as the other taxes no longer existed and the colonies were generally doing well economically. In addition, large numbers of colonists continued to boycott the tea. As a result, at first colonial politics and society largely returned to conducting business as usual.

Once again, however, British leaders and large financial interests chose to impose unwise trade policies on the colonies. In May 1773 Parliament passed an act allowing the British East India Company to bypass Britain and sell its tea directly to the American colonies at a reduced price. No added tax was involved. In turn, a number of colonial merchants and politicians called it a blatant attempt to lure Americans who were boycotting tea into buying it. That, of course, would force them to pay the existing tax on the tea.

This time, the protests in the colonies were bolder than ever. Local officials at the ports of New York, Philadelphia, and Charleston stopped the tea ships and told them to return to England. Most of the captains of these ships complied, but in Boston a more controversial scenario transpired. The royal governor, Thomas Hutchinson, refused to allow the tea ships to leave. To demonstrate their displeasure, on December 16, 1773, some local men dressed up as Indians, went to the docks, and threw 342 chests of tea into the harbor.

No one was injured in the incident, which became known as the "Boston Tea Party." However, back in England most

To protest a tax on tea, colonists dressed up as Indians and threw 342 chests of tea into the Boston Harbor on December 16, 1773. This act of defiance has become known as the "Boston Tea Party."

people were outraged by what they viewed as willful destruction of private property. Parliament reacted in what its members thought was an appropriate way—passing the Coercive Acts (called the Intolerable Acts in the colonies) between March and June 1774. These were meant to punish Boston by closing its port (until the residents paid for the lost tea); restricting the authority of the local assembly; and allowing the royal governor to quarter British troops in colonial homes.

British leaders expected the Coercive Acts to isolate Massachusetts and make an example of it. This, they hoped, would intimidate the other colonies and end resistance to British policies. However, the complete opposite occurred. The other colonies united in their support for the Boston "patriots," as locals who opposed British abuses increasingly called themselves. Defying Britain's blockade of that city, the colonies sent it thousands of tons of food and other relief supplies.

Another daring expression of colonial political unity took place on May 17, 1774. Eighty-nine members of the House of Burgesses (which only hours before had been dissolved by Virginia's governor for its support of Boston) met illegally in the Raleigh Tavern in Williamsburg. Present were some of the colony's leading politicians, including George Washington, Thomas Jefferson, and Patrick Henry. They drew up a document that read: "We are further clearly of [the] opinion, that an attack made on one of our sister colonies, to compel submission to arbitrary taxes, is an attack made on all British America, and threatens ruin to the rights of all, unless the united wisdom of the whole be applied."[64]

The Beginning of the End

The leading colonists' acceptance of this notion—that the colonies should and could be united in the causes of justice and freedom—proved to be the beginning of the end of British America. The following year, armed colonial farmers clashed with British redcoats at Concord and Lexington (villages outside of Boston) in the first battles of the American Revolution. On July 4, 1776, the colonies declared their independence from Britain, marking the birth of the United States.

Three main factors can be attributed to colonial politics and government reaching the point where rebellion from the mother country seemed to be the only viable option. First, there was the normal evolution of political thought and institutions one would expect in the course of a century and a half. The longer colonial legislatures worked to solve their own problems, the more they felt that they, and not Parliament, owned both the problems and the solutions. Second, the Enlightenment infused colonial political institutions and leaders with fresh, appealing concepts of liberal civil rights, equality, and justice. When Parliament seemed to run roughshod over these admirable concepts, the

The Colonies Pay Their Fair Share

Many colonists played active and important roles in the French and Indian War (1754–1763). Some provided economic support, while others actually fought alongside British troops. The colonists, therefore, felt they had contributed their fair share to waging and winning the conflict. Benjamin Franklin summed up this attitude in his 1766 interview by members of the House of Commons:

Commons: Do you think it right that America should be protected by this country and pay no part of the expense?

Franklin: That is not the case. The colonies raised, clothed, and paid [for] nearly 25,000 men [during the war] and spent many millions.

Commons: Were you not reimbursed by Parliament?

Franklin: We were only reimbursed what, in your opinion, we had advanced beyond our proportion, or beyond what might reasonably be expected from us; and it was a very small part of what we spent. Pennsylvania, in particular, disbursed about 500,000 [English pounds], and the reimbursements, in the whole, did not exceed 60,000 [pounds].

"Examination of Benjamin Franklin Before British House of Commons, February 13, 1766," in Richard B. Morris, ed., *The American Revolution, 1763–1783: A Bicentennial Collection.* Columbia: University of South Carolina Press, 1970, p. 82.

Speaking to the House of Commons in 1766, Benjamin Franklin relayed the colonists feeling that they had contributed to helping the British win the French and Indian War.

colonists grew increasingly angry and indignant.

Third, the great distance separating the colonies from Britain ensured that the two peoples would eventually grow apart. Thomas Paine's observation that Britain's attempt to run the colonies from across a vast ocean would "in a few years be looked upon as folly and childishness,"[65] came true with a vengeance. In what seemed a mere instant in the long march of European exploration and colonization, British colonial politics had become American politics.

Notes

Introduction: Shedding Past Traditions and Customs

1. Alan Taylor, *American Colonies: The Settling of North America.* New York: Penguin, 2001, p. 141.
2. "Frame of Government of Pennsylvania, May 5, 1782." Avalon Project. http://avalon.law.yale.edu/17th_century/pa04.asp.
3. Quoted in "John Winthrop." Spartacus Educational. www.spartacus.schoolnet.co.uk/USAwinthrop.htm.
4. Thomas Paine, *Common Sense.* Available at http://libertyonline.hypermall.com/Paine/CS-Body.html.

Chapter 1: Social Rank in British America

5. Jarret Devereaux, *The Autobiography of Jarret Devereaux,* in *William and Mary Quarterly,* Third Series, vol. 9, 1952, p. 361.
6. Quoted in *American Historical Review, vol. 3, October 1897–July 1898.* New York: Macmillan, 1898, p. 736.
7. Quoted in "John Winthrop."
8. Quoted in "John Winthrop."
9. Quoted in John C. Miller, *The First Frontier: Life in Colonial America.* Lanham, MD: University Press of America, 1986, p. 109.
10. Quoted in William Byrd, *A Journey in the Land of Eden, and Other Papers.* New York: Macy-Masius, 1928, p. 319.
11. Linda Baumgarten, "Colonial Dress Codes." Colonial Williamsburg. www.history.org/foundation/journal/winter03-04/clothing.cfm.
12. Quoted in John B. Dillon, *Oddities of Colonial Legislation.* Indianapolis: R. Douglas, 1879, pp. 27–28.
13. Taylor, *American Colonies,* pp. 311–12.
14. Baumgarten, "Colonial Dress Codes."
15. Miller, *The First Frontier,* p. 117.
16. "Virginia's James River Plantations: Westover." www.jamesriverplantations.org/Westover.html.
17. Taylor, *American Colonies,* p. 312.
18. Quoted in Alan Taylor, "Power Shopping, A Review of *The Marketplace and Revolution: How Consumer Politics Shaped American Independence.*" www.powells.com/review/2004_02_26.html.
19. William Smith, *The History of the Late Province of New York, from Its Discovery to the Appointment of Governor Colden in 1762.* New York: New York Historical Society, 1830, p. 332.

Chapter 2: Development of Colonial Government

20. "Charter of the Colony of New Plymouth." Avalon Project. http://avalon.law.yale.edu/17th_century/mass02.asp.

21. "The Mayflower Compact." Pilgrim Hall Museum. www.pilgrimhall.org/compact.htm.

22. "The Charter of Maryland." Lonang Library. www.lonang.com/exlibris/organic/1632-cm.htm.

23. Keith I. Polakoff et al., *Generations of Americans: A History of the United States*. New York: St. Martin's, 1985, p. 33.

24. "Fundamental Orders of Connecticut." Lonang Library. www.lonang.com/exlibris/organic/1639-foc2.htm.

25. Bernard Bailyn, "Colonial Government and Politics," in Eric Foner and John A. Garraty, eds., *The Reader's Companion to American History*. Boston: Houghton Mifflin, 1991, pp. 203–204.

26. Irwin Unger, *These United States: The Questions of Our Past*. Boston: Little, Brown, 2002, p. 60.

Chapter 3: The Impact of Bacon's Rebellion

27. Stephen S. Webb, *The End of American Independence*. Syracuse: Syracuse University Press, 1995, pp. xv–xvi.

28. Taylor, *American Colonies*, pp. 149–50.

29. "Robert Beverley on Bacon's Rebellion." www.vlib.us/amdocs/texts/beverley.html

30. Quoted in "Sir William Berkeley." www.sonofthesouth.net/revolutionary-war/british/sir-william-berkeley.htm

31. Samuel E. Morison, *The Oxford History of the American People: Vol. 1, Prehistory to 1789*. New York: Plume, 1994, p. 162.

32. Quoted in Morison, *The Oxford History of the American People*, p. 162.

33. "Robert Beverley on Bacon's Rebellion."

34. William Berkeley, *The Declaration and Remonstrance of Sir William Berkeley, His Most Sacred Majesties' Governor and Captain General of Virginia*. Available at: odur.let.rug.nl/~usa/D/1651-1700/bacon_rebel/berke.htm

35. Nathaniel Bacon, *The Declaration of the People*. Available at: odur.let.rug.nl/~usa/D/1651-1700/bacon_rebel/bacon.htm

36. Webb, *The End of American Independence*, p. 64.

37. Polakoff, *Generations of Americans: A History of the United States*, pp. 52–53.

Chapter 4: The Changing Social Status of Blacks

38. Quoted in Warren Billings, ed., *The Old Dominion in the 17th Century, A Documentary History of Virginia, 1606–1689*. Chapel Hill: University of North Carolina Press, 1975, p. 139.

39. Miller, *The First Frontier*, pp. 144–45.

40. Edward G. Gray, *Colonial America: A History in Documents*. New York: Oxford University Press, 2003, p. 98.

41. Gray, *Colonial America*, p. 84.

42. Quoted in Marion Tingling, ed., *The Correspondence of the Three William Byrds of Westover, Virginia, 1654–1776*, Vol. 1. Charlottesville: University Press of Virginia, 1977, p. 355.

43. Quoted in John B. Boles, *Black Southerners, 1619–1869*. Lexington: University Press of Kentucky, 1985, p. 23.

44. Quoted in Hugh Thomas, *The Slave Trade: The Story of the Atlantic Slave Trade, 1440–1870*. New York: Simon & Schuster, 1997, p. 431.

45. Quoted in Lathan A. Windley, *Runaway Slave Advertisements: A Documentary History from the 1730s to 1790*, Vol. 1. Westport, CT: Greenwood, 1983, p. 9.

Chapter 5: The Impact of the Enlightenment

46. "Seventeenth Century Enlightenment Thought." Washington State University, World Civilizations. www.wsu.edu/~dee/ENLIGHT/ENLIGHT.HTM.

47. Taylor, *American Colonies*, p. 446.

48. Cicero, *The Republic*, in *Cicero: The Republic and the Laws*, trans. Niall Rudd. New York: Oxford University Press, 1998, pp. 68–69.

49. John Locke, *The Second Treatise of Government*, ed. Thomas P. Peardon. Indianapolis: Bobbs-Merrill, 1952, p. 4.

50. Locke, *The Second Treatise of Government*, pp. 5–6.

51. Locke, *The Second Treatise of Government*, p. 128.

52. Murray N. Rothbard, "The Growth of Libertarian Thought in Colonial America." http://mises.org/content/cil2ch33.asp.

53. Quoted in Diane Ravitch and Abigail Thernstrom, eds., *The Democracy Reader*. New York: HarperCollins, 1992, p. 41.

54. James W. Davidson et al., *Nation of Nations: A Narrative History of the American Republic*. New York: McGraw-Hill, 1990, p. 140.

55. Henry S. Commager, "The Declaration of Independence," in Lally Weymouth, ed., *Thomas Jefferson: The Man, His World, His Influence*. London: Weidenfeld and Nicolson, 1973, p. 186.

Chapter 6: Growing Disputes with the Mother Country

56. Morison, *The Oxford History of the American People*, p. 248.

57. Taylor, *American Colonies*, p. 432.

58. Quoted in "Becoming American: The British Atlantic Colonies, 1690–1763." http://nationalhumanitiescenter.org/pds/becomingamer/american/text5/independence.pdf.

59. Quoted in Edmund S. Morgan and Helen M. Morgan, *The Stamp Act Crisis: Prologue to Revolution.* Chapel Hill, NC: University of North Carolina Press, 1995, p. 38.

60. Quoted in Max Beloff, ed., *The Debate on the American Revolution, 1761–1783.* London: Adam and Charles Black, 1960, p. 71.

61. "Examination of Benjamin Franklin Before British House of Commons, February 13, 1766," in Richard B. Morris, ed., *The American Revolution, 1763–1783: A Bicentennial Collection.* Columbia: University of South Carolina Press, 1970, p. 85.

62. George Grenville, "Speech to the British House of Commons, January 14, 1766," in Beloff, *Debate,* p. 98.

63. Samuel E. Morison, ed., *Sources and Documents Illustrating the American Revolution, 1764–1788, and the Formation of the Federal Constitution.* Oxford, Eng.: Clarendon Press, 1953, p. 53.

64. Quoted in Henry S. Commager and Richard B. Morris, eds., *The Spirit of 'Seventy-Six: The Story of the American Revolution as Told by Participants,* Vol. 1. New York: Bobbs-Merrill, 1958, p. 39.

65. Thomas Paine, *Common Sense.*

Time Line

1620
Separatists from England create a colony at Plymouth, in what is now Massachusetts.

1622–1683
Life of Algernon Sidney, an English Enlightenment thinker whose ideas are highly influential in colonial America.

1625
Dutch settlers establish the town of New Amsterdam (later New York City) on Manhattan Island.

1638
Connecticut's "Fundamental Orders of Government" are drawn up.

1648
Shah Jahan, emperor of India, erects the magnificent Taj Mahal as a monument to his deceased wife.

1674–1744
Life of William Byrd II, a Virginia aristocrat who typifies upper-class colonial values and privilege.

1676
Virginia's Nathaniel Bacon leads a bloody rebellion against that colony's government.

1690
English thinker John Locke publishes his *Two Treatises of Government*, a major document of the Enlightenment.

1691
A Virginia law states that the children of a white father and a black mother are not free.

1704
Virginia colonist and historian Robert Beverley writes an account of Bacon's Rebellion.

1706–1790
Life of Benjamin Franklin, one of the chief colonial American exponents of the Enlightenment.

1715
Rhode Island makes slavery legal.

1729
England's Carolina province splits into North and South Carolina.

1741
George Frideric Handel composes the famous choral work, *Messiah.*

1754–1763
The French and Indian War is fought in

North America by England and France.

1757
The British establish a strong presence in India.

1762
Catherine II (the Great) becomes ruler of Russia.

1765
Britain imposes the Stamp Act on its American colonies.

1776
Britain's thirteen North American colonies declare their independence from the mother country, thereby creating the United States.

For More Information

Books

Patricia U. Bonomi, *Under the Cope of Heaven: Religion, Society, and Politics in Colonial America*. New York: Oxford University Press, 2003. A detailed examination of the various ways that religion affected colonial American society.

Henry S. Commager, *The Empire of Reason: How Europe Imagined and America Realized the Enlightenment*. New York: Oxford University Press, 1982. This study by one of the leading American historians of the twentieth century effectively explores the ideas and influence of the Enlightenment.

Henry S. Commager and Richard B. Morris, eds., *The Spirit of 'Seventy-Six: The Story of the American Revolution as Told by Participants*, volume 1. New York: Bobbs-Merrill, 2002. A fulsome collection of original colonial documents, with excellent commentary by the editors.

Edward Countryman, *The American Revolution*. New York: Hill and Wang, 2003. Widely recognized as one of the greatest books ever written on the subject.

James Deetz and Patricia S. Deetz, *The Times of Their Lives: Life, Love, and Death in Plymouth Colony*. New York: Anchor, 2001. These first-rate schol-ars present a fresh, compelling, and well-documented look at the real history of Plymouth Colony.

Edward G. Gray, *Colonial America: A History in Documents*. New York: Oxford University Press, 2003. A useful collection of primary source documents about colonial America, with plenty of commentary by the editor.

Lucille Griffith, *Virginia House of Burgesses, 1750–74*. Tuscaloosa: University of Alabama Press, 1970. Follows the history of the Virginia legislature from early colonial days to the tense times preceding the American Revolution.

James Horn, *A Land as God Made It: Jamestown and the Birth of America*. New York: Basic, 2006. A fine scholar delivers one of the better existing studies of Jamestown and its importance to the colonial experience.

Michael G. Kammen, *Politics and Society in Colonial America*. Hinsdale, IL: Dryden Press, 1973. A good general overview of the subject.

Edmund S. Morgan and Helen M. Morgan, *The Stamp Act Crisis: Prologue to Revolution*. Chapel Hill, NC: University of North Carolina Press, 1995. One of the better studies of British taxation of the North American colonies and how dispute over that issue led the colonists to rebel against the mother country.

Samuel E. Morison, *The Oxford History of the American People: Vol. 1, Prehistory to 1789*. New York: Plume, 1994. Though now somewhat dated, this book by a great historian remains one of the best general overviews of American history.

Thomas L. Purvis, *Colonial America to 1763*. New York: Facts On File, 1999. Purvis has collected reams of statistics and lists of facts about colonial America here that provide detail and context for more general studies of the subject.

Alan Taylor, *American Colonies: The Settling of North America*. New York: Penguin, 2001. An extremely well-researched and nearly definitive treatment of the subject by a Pulitzer Prize–winning scholar.

Stephen S. Webb, *The End of American Independence*. Syracuse: Syracuse University Press, 1995. This extremely well-researched volume makes the case that Bacon's Rebellion and some early Indian wars were major turning points in colonial history.

Howard Zinn, *A People's History of the United States*. New York: Harper and Row, 2005. A contentious but thoughtful historian discusses some of the more controversial and shameful incidents and aspects of American history in this now classic volume.

Selected Internet Sources

Culpeper's Rebellion (www.learnnc.org/lp/editions/nchist-colonial/1979). A clearly-written, fact-filled overview of this influential event.

The House of Burgesses (www.socialstudiesforkids.com/articles/ushistory/houseofburgesses.htm). A brief but informational look at Virginia's early legislature.

Life in Colonial America (www.eastbuc.k12.ia.us/00_01/CA/home.htm). This site has many links to short, informative articles on various aspects of colonial society and its members.

Robert Beverley on Bacon's Rebellion (www.vlib.us/amdocs/texts/beverley.html). An excellent primary source, in which Beverley himself describes the rebellion.

Seventeenth-Century Documents (http://avalon.law.yale.edu/subject_menus/17th.asp). Contains links to several more important primary sources for the period and its events.

Seventeenth-Century Enlightenment Thought (www.wsu.edu/~dee/ENLIGHT/ENLIGHT.HTM). Click on "Resources" for many links to useful articles about the Enlightenment.

Index

Corporate colonies, 25–28
  revocation of charters of, 37
County, 34, 35–36
Culpepper's Rebellion, 48

D
Declaration of Independence, *67,* 70
Dickinson, John, 78–79
Discourses Concerning Government
  (Sidney), 64
Dress/dress codes, social rank and,
  18–21
Drummond, William, 59

E
Eddis, William, 20
Electorate, colonial, 34–35
Eliot, Andrew, 64
Elson, Henry W., 33
England
  development of parliamentary system
    in, 9–10
  intervention in colonial rebellions,
    37–38
English Bill of Rights (1689), 9
Enlightenment, 60–61
  basis of, 61–62
  contribution to American Revolution,
    81
  in Europe, 63–65, 66–67
  right to liberty and, 62–63
  spread of ideas of in colonies, 70
Ethics (Aristotle), 66

F
Franklin, Benjamin, 67–68, 76–77, 82,
  82
French and Indian War (1754–1763),
  73–74, 82

G
George III (King of England), 74
Governors, colonial, 30, 32
Gray, Edward G., 52, 54–55
Grenville, George, 77

H
Hamilton, Dr. Alexander, 22–23
Happiness, 68–71
Henry, Patrick, 81
Homes/housing, 21
Hooker, Richard, 60
House of Lords (England), *31*
Hutcheson, Francis, 64
Hutchinson, Thomas, 79

I
Indentured servants, 13, 16, 35, 49,
  52
  decrease in numbers of, 52
Intolerable Acts (Coercive Acts, 1774),
  81

J
Jamestown, 25, 33, 72
  Bacon's Rebellion in, 45–46, *46*
  first African slaves arriving at, *50*
  House of Burgesses meeting in, *35*
Jarret, Deveraux, 13–14
Jefferson, Thomas, 13, 63, 68, 70, 81

K
King Philip's War (1675–1676), 47,
  48

L
Legislatures, 32–34
Liberty
  division of government and, 66–67

Picture Credits

About the Author

Historian and award-winning author Don Nardo has written many books for young adults about American history; among them *The Salem Witch Trials, The Sons of Liberty, The Declaration of Independence, The Mexican-American War,* and *The Great Depression*; biographies of presidents Thomas Jefferson, Andrew Johnson, and Franklin D. Roosevelt; several volumes about Native American history and culture; and a survey of the weapons and tactics of the American Revolution. Mr. Nardo lives with his wife Christine in Massachusetts.